Telep

HOURS OF OPEI
TERM TIME
VACATIONS 9

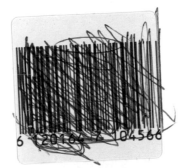

VICTORIAN CAMERAMAN

Francis Frith's Views of
Rural England 1850–1898

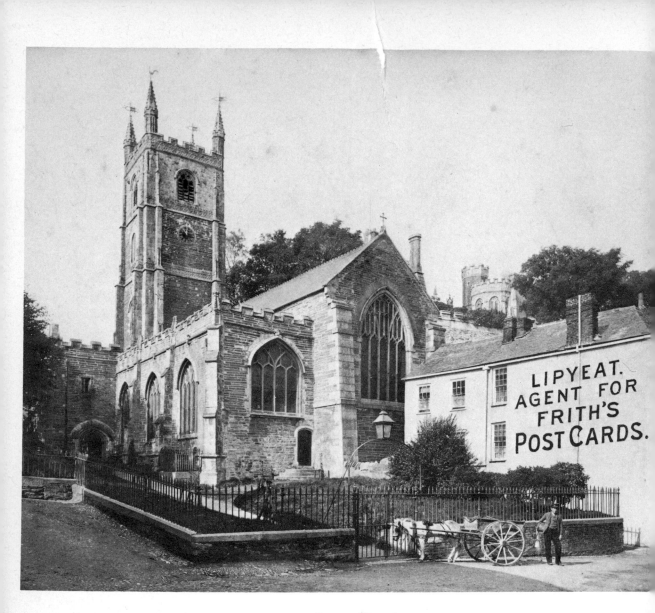

Fowey Church

VICTORIAN CAMERAMAN

Francis Frith's Views of
Rural England 1850~1898

Written and Edited by Bill Jay

David & Charles: Newton Abbot

0 7153 5895 2

Set in 11/12pt Modern by C. E. Dawkins (Typesetters) Ltd London SE1
and printed in Great Britain
by The Pitman Press Bath
for David & Charles (Holdings) Limited
South Devon House Newton Abbot Devon

Contents

The Francis Frith Collection which is featured in this book has been purchased by Rothmans of Pall Mall, London.

As the collection is of such outstanding historical interest and is certainly a unique record of Victorian England, it is the intention of Rothmans to restore the whole collection. It will also be comprehensively indexed and, from time to time, exhibited throughout the country.

'a truthful record is of more value
than the most elaborately beautiful picture'

Introduction to Francis Frith photographs in
Cairo, Sinai, Jerusalem and the Pyramids of Egypt, 1860

Introduction

As a photographic enthusiast with a particular interest in Victorian documentary photographers, I was naturally aware of Francis Frith's travels in Egypt and Palestine. Volumes of these pictures are in the British Museum, in the Royal Photographic Society Permanent Collection, in the George Eastman House in Rochester, New York, and in many other major collections of photography. I was also aware of Frith's postcard factory, but I had never seen original examples of Frith's photographs of rural and urban England. Not, that is, until 4 February, 1971.

A few days before that date, I had received a telephone call from a friend at Time-Life Books, Margot Hapgood, who informed me that Francis Frith & Co was now in liquidation and, knowing my interest in the photography of that period, perhaps I would like to visit the factory and buy some old postcards before they were thrown out. I must admit that the prospect of a drive into the country with a pub lunch attracted me more than the postcards.

However, on arrival, it soon became apparent, much to my surprise and delight, that the original prints, from which the postcards were made, were still in existence. In fact it was difficult to ignore the fact. They filled several rooms, stacked in their hundreds of thousands in boxes that lined the walls from floor to ceiling. They were unmounted and, therefore, in exceptionally good condition. On many subsequent visits, I bought as many of the prints as my meagre finances allowed. When it became apparent that the remaining prints would be frittered away, or even burnt, on the winding up of the company, I made every effort to find a purchaser for the entire collection. Eventually, in the last possible week of business before the staff was dismissed and the building sold, the firm of Rothmans, Pall Mall, London, gave me the authority to act on their behalf and negotiate a price for all the original prints and remaining glass plates. I say 'remaining', for although art museums are culpable in failing to preserve this unique record of the previous century, Frith's company must bear an equally large share of the blame. A few years ago, its employees smashed with hammers thousands of the earliest, pre-1886, and now extremely valuable, glass plates and mixed the pieces with concrete to make the floor of an outhouse. A week before the demolition of the company's Reigate headquarters, a photographic's student, John Lawrence Jones, was browsing through the garden when he found a solid wall of glass, about ten yards long and two to three feet deep and wide, comprising thousands upon thousands of Frith's original glass plates. The wall was covered in bracken and top soil, but many of the plates, including some 16×20in Egyptian views, still contained beautiful images. Unfortunately, exposure to dirt and rain over many years had ruined the emulsions beyond salvation.

Although a complete inventory has not been made, I would estimate that the remaining Frith collection comprises at least 60,000 original glass plates and 250,000 original prints. The plates were stored in rotting tin boxes in a damp basement and a wooden, outdoor shack; the prints in filthy card boxes that tended to disintegrate on handling. Yet the vast majority are in excellent condition, considering many of them are over 100 years old.

The collection saved, I began in earnest to discover more about this remarkable man who had bequeathed us the most extensive, important and well-preserved collection of British documentary photography to have survived more or less intact. The results of this search appear as the text of this book. If I am confident that most of this information is published for the first time and is unknown even to photographic historians; I am less than confident that I have done justice to the material. The words published between these covers account for only a part of the, to me fascinating, information that could have been written about the tenacious, adventurous, supremely self-confident photo-grapher, this typical Victorian middle-class family man, this complex philosopher and poet.

I have tried to present a rounded portrait of Francis Frith, fleshed out with details of all aspects of his life and career, coloured with anecdotes from his own writings, touched up with reminiscences from the surviving members of his family. The photographic historian will find much scholarly research is missing: the layman may find many of the details irrelevant. I can only say, in the words of Francis Frith himself:

I have, however, one consolidation, viz., that if the critics will be good enough not to call disagreeable attention to my writings, not one person in ten will think of looking at it. Scarcely any one ever *does* read the letter press which accompanies a series of views, any more than one thinks of scrutinising the 'gold sticks' who shuffle, as a matter of course, after a royal pageant . . . I am perfectly content that my own descriptive matter should thus be considered as entirely subordinate to my views.

Francis Frith

Francis Frith
1822~1898

COUNTRY BOY-HOOD

He was born in 1822 at Chesterfield in Derbyshire, 'a pretty country town, as stagnant as one of those secluded fish-ponds of the last century, that were full of rank greenery, and lazy, insipid carp and tench—and as interesting to boys.'

His father was a cooper whose ancestors had lived for generations in and near this midland-counties town. One of his beautifully-made miniature barrels, about 9ins high, with alternate stripes of dark and light woods, is still in the Frith family. Francis was proud of the fact that there were records of the Friths in that area for over two hundred years. It was one of these ancestors who made a decision which was profoundly to affect the attitudes and life-style of Francis himself. George Fox, the Quaker preacher, was 'hospitably entertained' by one of them, who became his convert; and the family appeared to have remained staunch members of the sect down until Francis' time. There was a brief lapse when his father married a lady who was of the 'outer world'. A pretty miniature shows her in early life, with an abundance of coquettish, light-brown curls and a fashionable short-

Chesterfield, Derbyshire

Chesterfield Church

sleeved and short-waisted bodice which would have been considered frivolous by the pious and dour Quakers. According to the rigid practice of that day, his father was 'disowned' for 'marrying out'. But he was soon readmitted, along with his converted wife, 'who ever afterwards evinced a sincere attachment to her husband's people.'

Francis' father was a well educated man. As befitted a staunch Quaker lad, he was sent to Ackworth school, the intellectual nursery of the Society of Friends. There he learnt to write and spell faultlessly—'which is more than some university men can do.' Many pupils at Ackworth did not see their parents for periods of four or five years,

though Frith's father would probably have travelled home for the holidays, as the school was only 35 miles from Chesterfield. Francis' father was well read in the English classics, and liked to quote Shakespeare 'with much dramatic effect'. He was fond of art, and was himself a good draughtsman; 'but it was morally and religiously that he was grand. He was a great and intelligent student of the Bible.'

Francis Frith had two sisters; the elder died at the age of fifteen, when Francis was thirteen. He remembered her as 'a singularly lovely and fine-souled girl. I am at this moment looking forward with intense interest to meeting her, and renewing our too brief acquaintance, in the after-life.' Apart from this tragic death, 'my first vision of the great and awful figure of Sorrow', Francis seems to have had an idyllic childhood.

> The memories of my boyhood are very largely of fields and streams and green lanes, of rabbit holes and bird's nests and minnows. The village school-mistress in her spectacles, and even the 'Reverend' Domine who succeeded her, with his massive head, and sallow thoughtful face, and his cane across the desk, are shadowy forms, compared with that of a certain gigantic pear-tree in my father's garden, amid whose branches I spent many a rare unbrageous hour, and innumerable bits of picturesque hill and dale where I wandered and fished and 'muttered my wayward fancies' through long summer days of half unconscious happiness, drinking in at every pore of nerve and soul the poetry of nature, and nursing into wild and vigorous growth, under conditions the most absolutely favourable to them, every inborn faculty of person and mind that I can recognise as specialities of my constitution.

> The town of my nativity had a fine old church with a wonderful spire, a good deal out of the perpendicular. I have no doubt that spire has twisted itself vigorously into my mental frame, for I was generally sent by my Mother, for a run before breakfast, to see if it had fallen. There was a great open market-place which attracted on fair-days the elite of showmen and tumblers and cheap-Johnnies. There were miles, as it seems to me, of ginger-bread stalls, and toys and cheap crockery ornaments. There I saw too

a pig-faced lady whose face and form are far more vivid in my memory than are those of thousands of beautiful women whom I have since beheld. The peculiar wild-beast smell of Woombell's Menagerie is fresh in my nostrils, the mangy hyena still occasionally shows me his teeth, and a huge bald-headed stork that walked about the menagerie loose, gingerly picking up his sticks of legs and winking knowingly at the public, has always been associated in my mind with certain dried up and wise-looking men whom I have occasionally met in my 'walk through life'.

This description of boyhood in a Quaker family of the 1820s is clearly at odds with the impression of dour drabness often associated with the early Society of Friends. Francis Frith was also aware of the disparity in images. 'Not only has it (Quakerism) not, nor ever had, any of the repulsive and ascetic character which novelist and persons ignorant of the matter have attributed to it, but . . . the doctrines and principles of the Society were even then, in liberality and foresight, in advance even of the average religious intelligences of the present day (1884).' Frith describes the atmosphere of religion in his time as 'strict not sour'.

He was conscious that he 'undoubtedly sinned now and then, very grievously.' This harsh self-inflicted judgement was for telling 'a few terrible "stories" ', secretly dipping into the 'sugar and meal' bowl, and taking 'a knife from my father's desk, with the full intention, if I hadn't broken or lost it, of restoring it.' By the time he was nine, young Francis had had the usual narrow escapes from injury. He was knocked down by the leading horse of a coach and spun just beyond the track of the wheels. For some reason, this escape earned Francis a beating with a door-mat from his father. Francis also remembered being attacked and savaged by a powerful dog which managed to drag him into its kennel before he could be pulled away by the heels.

If Francis ever found fault with his parents it was that they smothered him with 'a painfully heavy load' of self-sacrificing love. 'It is scarcely fair to a child, and certainly not for his comfort or good, that parents should live so ostensibly only for their offspring, half forgetting what they owe to themselves and to society.'

SCHOOL-DAYS

It is not surprising that this tranquil boyhood, cossetted with affection, was rudely shattered by boarding school. Between 1834 and 1838 Francis attended the Quaker Camp Hill school in Birmingham.

> Nothing, surely, but a good stock of animal spirits, and youthful carelessness of the 'inalienable rights of mankind' can make boys happy under the iron tyranny and taskwork of boarding-school life. To me, now, the precincts of an Academy are odious. I had nearly as soon enter a prison as a young gentleman's Seminary. If I have a nightmare, I dream of going back to school.
>
> Boarding-school and its period of life is the most insipid and mechanical portion of existence, and it is not nearly so effective in the formation of character as the earlier home influence. I have rarely or never known a youth greatly, indeed scarcely perceptibly, altered in character by his career at school . . . My own schoolfellows at fifty are merely exaggerated caricatures of what they were at ten . . . one boy was full of genuine wit and of quaint sayings and yet a dunce at his lessons, another as reckless and wild as any young 'blood' or 'man about town' of the last generation, a third a born artist . . . The dunce turned out a first rate man of business, a shrewd, useful man, loved and respected. The rove soon ran through a fortune, and killed himself by excess, and the artist won fame and fortune with his brush; and *so* without exception of the rest.

At sixteen, Francis Frith started his career. He had reached a fair standard in Latin, though his Greek was poor and his French never rose above the conversational. He was better at English, mathematics and natural philosophy. He read poetry 'with keen delight' and enjoyed travel books and biographies. As soon as he escaped systematic study he went 'head over ears' into meta-

Colmore Row, Birmingham

physics, which 'doubtless trained my reasoning faculty, stimulated my imagination and enriched my mind in some directions but left me grievously deficient in exact, general, and polite knowledge, a deficiency which I have bitterly regretted in later life.'

Francis' father had now left business and was living in an old country farmstead 'done up' with verandahs and trellis-work. For the next few months Francis lived the life of a young loafer. He explored the countryside, learned to shoot rabbits, snipe and woodcock, and to ride a shaggy little horse 'self-willed and lazy. He, if I took him into a pond to drink, dropped down, before or behind, I know not, and, leaving me in the water, trotted cheerfully home.' He learned some of the mysteries of gardening and farming and studied rural science. Not all was peaceful. His guns tended to explode unprompted; a powder-flask burst in his hand, while he was meditatively dribbling its contents into a fire.

APPRENTICESHIP

These were happy, if not very profitable times—his life's holiday. But it soon came to an end. His parents moved to Sheffield to make a home for him during his five years apprenticeship in a cutlery firm. His father paid a good premium, boarded him and Francis served his time 'with a hearty, self-sacrificing vengeance.' His master, a well-read batchelor, 'notwithstanding that he fell a prey to the shabby custom of the times, and took my father's money and my long and faithful service as a matter of right', could be generous. Although not wealthy, he would 'toss a £500 cheque to a cause that interested him.' Francis Frith recalled that he 'reaped no benefit from my long years of hard and faithful labour, except a glowing testimonial on the flyleaf of an illustrated book, and I had learned nothing that was of further value to me except the art of steady, hard work, and the mechanical trick of posting ledgers and casting up figures.'

Yet these five years were not wasted; for outside work hours, he read all the poetry, philosophy, theology and science that he could lay his hands on. He wrote a number of poems. One of the earliest, written when he was only seventeen, was called 'Lines, written after parting from a young lady, then suffering from illness.'

> Oft have I left thee bright and clear, my first
> blue summer sky!
>   With the starlight beaming from thy brow or
>   the sunbeam from thine eye,
> And ever when I left thee, through the winter of
> my woe;
>   The starlight and the sunbeam would alternate
>   come and go.
> Oft have I left thee smiling, whilst the charmed
> air around
>   Exchanged the smile for music of a soft
>   ecstatic sound;
> O gaily danced the light of love o'er my tranced
> spirit then

The remainder has been lost, as has the rest of his writing of this period, except a passionate poem written in the same year, 1839, called 'Reform'. Not all his writings were poetic; during his apprenticeship, he spent much time and mental effort on religious and metaphysical essays. He was very interested in mechanical science devising and constructing various models, including a rotary steam-engine. 'This of course ended in scientific failure and in financial disaster.' But he was exploring his own talents, increasing his faculty for turning his hand to various and widely different occupations, experimenting with life's possibilities. He felt: 'To be a man of but one idea or one accomplishment is a very sorry distinction, and a still worse foundation for personal happiness.'

These five years presented Frith with a turmoil of new experiences. He met widely different people, including an obviously attractive and, for a while, successful sinner. But the Quaker in him 'set his teeth firmly' against the friendship, and he noted later that 'He came to awful grief, I think to the gallows at last.' New concepts, new friends, new values, new skills; and this at a period when he was experiencing the internal tensions of transition from adolescence to manhood. These bewildering changes caused a physical and mental breakdown. Frith wrote of this period:

> It resembles the moment in a hunter's life when, after infinite pains, and weary watching to find his game, it faces him at last in the moonlight, huge and indistinct and terrible, and he draws the trigger upon which his very life depends. Such was the tension of my mind and soul as I approached the close of my five years 'toil at the oar' of business life . . . My health, which had never been robust, broke down under the strain, and my nervous system, always highly strung, shook me with a pitiless energy which threatened both life and reason.

He was twenty-one years of age.

Francis spent the next couple of years travelling around England, Wales and Scotland with his parents. Recovery was tedious. But this period of relaxation not only restored his health, it marked a turning point in his spiritual life. His intellectual predilections for Quakerism were crystallised into a personal faith; he no longer merely believed, he lived his Christianity. Fully recovered, he looked around for 'something to do.'

BUSINESS—GREEK RAISINS AND PRINTING

He moved to Liverpool and began a wholesale grocery business, in partnership with a young man 'of fine principles and a most amiable disposition.' For the next few years

> we jogged on together on friendly terms, toiling at our daily drudgery with that wonderful, persistent, tick-tack mixture of hopelessness and resignation which animates a town clock. It must have been a weary struggle! But we soon separated amicably, and I then worked hard,

Lime Street and St George's Hall, Liverpool

and established a fine profitable business. But it was anxious and terribly wearing work. With inadequate capital, I turned over some £200,000 a year, and, after a few years, sold the concern on favourable terms to my principal opponents (I was about thirty-four years of age), retiring with a moderate fortune.

This account by Frith poses some awkward problems in reconstructing the chronology of his life. If he was thirty-four on selling his grocery business, this would make the year 1856. But we know from several reliable sources that he had started a printing company in 1850. Even if we assume that the memory of the elderly Frith was mistaken in believing he was about thirty-four when he sold the business, this would mean that he only worked for five years to achieve a turnover of £200,000, since the earliest year in which he could have started the business was 1845. This seems unlikely even taking

into account his cornering the Greek raisin crop!

I believe that the sentence 'But we soon separated amicably, and I then worked hard, and established a fine and profitable business' compresses too much time into too few words, and is therefore ambiguous. I suspect that the grocery business was never very successful, and that when the partnership was dissolved after five years, the business ceased to exist. So when Frith says '. . . and I then worked hard, and established a fine and profitable business' he is not talking about groceries but about a *new* business, his printing company. This explanation would mean that Frith was a printer for six years, from 1850 to 1856. This fits in with all the other facts about Frith's life which I have been able to uncover, except one. We shall see later that Frith's photographic business

14

claimed that it was established in 1850—but how could it have been if that was the company that was sold in 1856? Once again, we must speculate. I believe Frith started taking photographs first as an amateur, but later, in 1850, for sale. This would have been a separate business from the printing company, though a useful adjunct to it. Therefore, on restarting his photographic and printing business in Reigate, Surrey, in 1859, he could reasonably claim that his activities were begun in 1850.

WEALTH AND LEISURE

Before we return to this three year gap, between the selling of his printing business in 1856 and the start of his Reigate firm in 1859, it is interesting to read Frith's own comments on business life:

> . . . the necessity to labour is no curse; but the spirit in which money earning work is done is very often and very largely a cursing spirit. It may easily become a means of crushing out the little germ of generous, true, spiritual life and noble aspiration which God and nature have planted in a man. That it actually does complete the moral and even the intellectual degredation of thousands, no thoughtful person can doubt. There is nothing even in commercial success that any man need be proud of. Some of the poorest, most ignorant and most vulgar minds make 'capital, shrewd, successful business men' . . . There is an amazing amount of deceit and untruthfulness in trade . . . it is a sordid, low, vulgar, spiritual condition, a life of menial toil and drudgery upon a narrow polluted stream . . . the mechanical money-making portion of ten or twelve years of my life which preceded my marriage, I regard it as an utter blank . . . it constitutes no part of my real life during that period . . . The necessity for close attention to business—and a necessity it was, or I should soon have been commercially ruined—left me little time for study or reading. Thus no doubt it directly impoverished my mind, and, in all probability it tended, in some degree, to divert me from that absorbing devotion to religious thought and study to which I was strongly inclined . . . I had throughout a profound contempt for the commercial mind, pure and simple, and a horror of having my soul murdered in the

moral purlieus of the haunts of trade. It was no merit in me that I never thirsted after wealth; my disposition was rather to underate the value of temporal possessions and to hold them too lightly when earned.

If Francis Frith found money-making distasteful and time wasting, he seemed no better suited to leisure. Retiring in early manhood from his business career, he rented a fine old mansion near London, and for a year or two led the life of a country gentleman. 'This again,' he said 'was, for the most part, an aimless and unprofitable spell of existence upon which I look back with little satisfaction'. Leading a solitary and meditative sort of life, he fell back upon books and art, nature and poetry. They were days of careless ease. His, now elderly, parents were living with him.

He decided to travel, not Westwards to America as so many of his fellows were doing,

Francis Frith

15

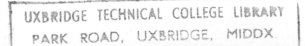

but eastwards, to Asia and Africa, Arabia and Palestine. Before 1860 he had made three separate tours of these countries, 'following my quest towards the romantic and perfected past, rather than to the bustling and immature present.'

On his first journey, lasting from September 1856 to July 1857, he travelled up the Nile valley, viewing the monuments from Cairo to Abu Simbel. In November 1857, he left England again, after a stay of only three months. This time he journeyed around Palestine and Syria, visiting Jerusalem, Damascus, Mount Sinai and Baalbek; places that were known to the Victorians only by their fabulous reputations. This second trip lasted until May 1858, after which Frith spent more than a year in England. But in the summer of 1859, he began his third and last expedition, which was to lead over 1,500 miles up the Nile and was to establish his reputation.

EXPEDITIONS TO EGYPT
The voyage from Liverpool to Alexandria was:

a perilous one, in a rolling, wall sided, nearly new screw-ship, seven times the length of her beam. We had a tremendous gale of wind nearly the whole way, but fair, doing an average with sail and steam of fifteen knots *on the flat*, and half as much again if you reckon the ups and down of the tremendous billows. Many a time half the ship's length was covered with a flood of water which she scooped up with her nose in the trough of the wave and tossed backward, when she rose, as by a miracle, quivering in every nerve. When we reached the bar of the harbour, upon which, in fair weather, through a narrow channel, there is only just about depth of water to float a big ship—there was no pilot out! He is pretty certain death to those men if they escape the sea and cannot conceal themselves on shore, after losing a ship.

A subsequent attempt to enter the Nile was equally fraught with danger. Frith had brought from England a little high-pressure steam-launch. Since the only navigable channel into the Nile in those days was over

sixty miles away, over the bay, he attempted, without a pilot, to find a way into the Rosetta mouth of the Nile. The steam launch was dropped from the deck of the mother ship into the harbour at Alexandria:

It is five o'clock on a beautiful calm morning in June. The heart of the Arab pilot who had [been] engaged to accompany us, fails him. We steam to sea, trusting to our own look-out. We cross the bay successfully. Then about noon, we approach as we suppose the mouth of the river. We see nothing however but a wall of angry white breakers, stretching as far as the eye can reach. The sea is rising. Our little high pressure boiler is nearly saturated with salt. The engineer has just told us that it is useless to think of returning when a great wave strikes us and sweeps the foredeck. I rush to the helm, turn her head to the sea, and she rides gallantly. But what to do? To run into that wall of angry water is surely madness. See! There above the top of it, is the point of a lateen sail. It is but a narrow wall of water. On the other side of it doubtless flows the tranquil current of the Nile. If we delay, we are lost at sea. To dive into the breakers is almost a certain death. But if we *must* perish, we will at least have done our best. So pull up all the canvas, put on all the steam, and steer right into the surf! It is an awful moment. Our Arab dragoman wrings his hands and weeps but you and I and our English sailor are as cool and collected as if nothing were amiss. We know the strong probability is that we shall be drowned in five minutes time. I suppose it was the life or death necessity of the moment which strung my nerves so that I steered as steadily as I ever did in my life into what appeared to be inviolable destruction. Now we are into it! A wave has leaped upon us, shattering into a cloud of heavy spray, and rushing into our little saloon. Another! We are half full . . . A third wave is upon us. It strikes the gauge glass. Out comes the steam like thunder. We are at the mercy of the waves! But even *they* have mercy. At each stroke whilst they fill us they lift us like a cork and hurl us forward. Hastily we throw overboard coals, tackle, anything to lighten her. She strikes! We are safe! Overboard now. Everybody. Never mind the seas! Here comes a wave—now for a push. On she goes again—she is in the Nile!

Alexandria was 'the greatest sensation that I had ever experienced.' He wrote thousands of words about his adventures in the Middle

East, and his scrawling pen covered pages of manuscript, none of which, to my knowledge, have ever been published. They make fascinating reading. He tells of his months of exploration, 'fearing no evil, amongst men whom we call real savages, men whose naked bodies were unctuous with oil, and their matted hair frizzed out to a diameter of a couple of feet, and stuck through with arrows.' These 'creatures' may have lacked most of the graces of conventional civilisation but in Frith's eyes they were also free from 'some of its conspicuous vices, and whose souls appear to be, if anything, rather more religiously enlightened than is the soul of an average, modern, scientific professor.'

He spent a sweltering summer in Cairo, passing the nights on board ship, the only place where he could find relief from the burning heat, which on occasions rose to 110°F. He tried living in a tomb at the foot of the Great Pyramid, but had to fight a midnight battle, 'to the very point of exhaustion and surrender', with a deadly pack of hungry wild dogs. He spent six weeks bargaining with a 'mysterious priest who visited me by night' for a splendid illuminated copy of the Koran. The priest eventually accepted one-sixth of the original price. This seven-volume Koran, exquisitely drawn and coloured is over 800 years old and is, perhaps, the finest copy in Europe. It is now in the British Museum, with a penciled credit: 'Donated by a clergyman'. Frith was not an ordained minister, but he was a travelling preacher for the Society of Friends.

As he sailed out of Cairo on a passenger boat, he leaned over the rails and pulled his favourite watch, a silver Hunter, from his pocket. While opening the lid, it slipped from his hand and fell into the river. He made a careful note of its location and when he returned, he hired a dragoman and some boys to dive for it. The search was successful and the watch, which still keeps good time, now belongs to a grandson.

Manuscript of Frith's writings on the Middle East

Frith could not stop trading. He invested in Arab horses. He bargained with a sheikh of the Sinai Arabs for six or eight baggage camels and a safe conduct for forty days through Sinai and 'long desert' to the borders of Palestine. He met with desert princes 'blazing with jewelled-hilted swords and gold-mounted firearms'. Choosing a hitherto untrodden route, he was captured by robbers. He bargained, this time for his

The boat in which Francis Frith travelled up to the Second Cataract of the Nile

release, and after a 'noisy sham fight' the thieves escaped in the night carrying off his cooking utensils! Having escaped a 'rude mobbing' in Gaza, by the help of a Turk, he travelled on by donkey through Hebron, 'poking about' among the ruins, until he reached Jerusalem. 'Jerusalem . . . the greenly city . . . crowned—but fearfully desolate! Holy and beautiful, but terribly debased and defiled! Nineteen times destroyed, but indestructable!' Pitching his tent against the ancient walls, he set about exploring every part of the city, above and below ground. He lived in a stone built fortress on the Mount of Olives, blockading it against an arab band from the Jericho valley. They were 'atrocious looking bandits who had recently murdered or carried off a European or two (one of them a lady) for ransom, and who after reconnoitring me

thoroughly, seemed to "think better of it." ' They did eventually steal his ammunition while he was out on a field trip, leaving him enough, however, to bag three or four brace of partridges on his way 'home'.

Travelling from Jericho, via the Jordan Valley and the Dead Sea, he reached the plain of Esdraelan, where he was yet again set upon by robbers, but they 'vainly tried their noisy demands against our quiet, non-resistant, disconcerting composure.' And so his adventures continued. A leopard carried off a lamb from close to his tent near Tiberias; his groom was struck by fever so Frith carried him to a native physician, who gave him a bag of seeds to lie on, and a bottle of beetles to gaze at, 'whereupon he recovered'; his tent was carried off by still more robbers, followed by Frith in his night costume who 'recovered the spoil after a

18

gallant chase'. He continued on mule back, through the Lebanon, to Jaffa where he boarded a French steamer for Alexandria. From there he went to the Bosphorus, Constantinople, Smyrna and the Isles of Greece.

On the third expedition, Frith travelled by boat, horse and camel above the Sixth Cataract, over 1,500 miles from the Nile Delta, further than any photographer had been before (he claimed to be the second white man to have explored the Nile up to this point). This was a dozen years before the famous meeting between Stanley and Livingstone. In Frith's time few travellers ventured above the Second Cataract, which could be reached by boat. He had hired a team of Arabs to carry his craft up and over the cliffs alongside the falls, a manoeuvre which he described as 'a weary provoking business—a piece of unmitigated Arab trickery'. He was even provoked into writing a scathing poem about his helpers, the last two verses of which read:

And against the world of humbug may be
    confidently backed
That notorious ascending of the famous Cataract:
When all the tottering weak old men, and little
    mothers' hopes
To swell the poor imposture, are assembled at
    the ropes.

They sit for hours among the rocks, and leave
    you there for days
To magnify their services by pitiful delays
They give your boat a bump or two, to show how
    you may rue it.
Unless you fee them handsomely and pay them
    not to do it.

Above the Second Cataract Francis Frith continued his journey by dromedary, travelling light except for his bulky photographic equipment. Escorted by his dragoman, cook, boy and two guides he reached the Sixth Cataract in eighteen days. It is important to stress the fact that Frith did indeed travel beyond the Sixth Cataract, since photographic historians have unanimously

restricted his achievement to the Fifth. Frith himself wrote:

I had an exciting dromedary ride of thirty miles into the heart of the desert above the Sixth Cataract upon the tracks of a panther and an antelope . . . The fine spiral horns of the latter adorn my hall. My slippers often rest uneasily upon a Turkey hearth rug—in vexation that is not a panther skin: it is better that *that* skin is not beautified with an extra spot (or) does not at this moment parade the desert with a sleeker gloss and a prouder mien through enrichment of the blood and bones of a foolhardy Englishman!

Frith had his qualms about hunting. However, he recalled how the pigeons had been so numerous along the Nile, that on one occasion three barrels, simultaneously fired, brought down fifty-eight birds. He even shot crocodile, but was not enamoured of

Arab sportsman and cook

There's a sentiment stay-at-home people have learned
To a beautiful air to sing
Which at least as far as I am concerned
Is not exactly the thing:—
'Mid pleasures and palaces tho' we may roam'
'There's no place,' they tell us,' there's no place like home'

Now the fact is, wherever I happen to be
And chance such a thing to need.
The place that is not a "home" to me
Must be a poor place indeed.
Round my heart a hundred memories throng
With a home in each sweet enough for a song.

I have homes of my boyhood, sugary sweet,
By streams and in forest glades
No feet but my own and fairy feet
Have trod those sacred shades.
Nobody else the waterfall sees!
Nobody else can find the trees!

I have homes of my youth upon craggy heights
That look over the far blue sea
And parks that are mine by spirit-rights.
Whose ever else they may be
I have country seats and boxes by scores
On Derbyshire heaths and Perthshire moors!

Manuscript of poem

its flesh: 'I have eaten crocodile chops in various ways—fried and boiled and curried—but am not yet a convert to the diet. It is toughish white meat rather like veal with a flavour of musk.'

But Frith's main delight was in the ruins —temples, sphinxes, pyramids, tombs, rock carvings and sculptures. His writings are littered with awe-filled descriptions of them, and they are the subjects of the vast majority of his photographs.

Yet he could also observe these lands with

the eyes of a Victorian empire builder. 'It is an exciting thought that perhaps to England will eventually fall the task of governing this wonderful land, and of reviving and Christianising its mummied and paralysed life'.

But Frith, the Englishman, was able to criticise and he felt his countrymen certainly deserved criticism for their Egyptian policy.

. . . almost all the political influence is French. France, mainly by her superior consular tact and management has acquired a vast prestige in the East. Even the engineering supremacy of England will receive a severe blow when M. Lesseps shall have completed his Suez Canal, which England from motives of political jealousy so long persisted in ridiculing and declaring impossible. But it is diverting to observe with what proud and silent indifference English travellers regard this undisguised preference—so long as the oriental serves his purpose or stands out of his way the travelling Englishman cares not a straw what else is thought or done in the East.

The Suez Canal was begun in 1866 and completed in 1869. Frith has pencilled through the second sentence in the original manuscript, perhaps assuming that his private opinions would be too strong for his lecture audience. Frith was not to know that the British government, under Disraeli, would later buy a controlling interest in the Canal, in 1875.

He called his last trip 'a feat, and perhaps a folly', for between expeditions he had fallen in love. She was young and he had wanted 'one more grand spell of sunshine, and so finally brace up soul and body for the great events of life'. As he sailed homeward to England and marriage, he wrote this poem, which he described as a 'genuine unlaboured expression of the feelings of the moment':

There's a sentiment stay-at-home people have
  learned
  To a beautiful air to sing,
Which, at least so far as I am concerned,
  Is not exactly the thing:
'Mid temples and places though we may roam,

There's no place', they tell us, 'there's no place
    like home'.
Now the fact is, wherever I happen to be,
    And chance such a thing to need,
The place that is *not* a home to me
    Must be a strange place indeed!
Over mountains or deserts, wherever I roam,
Be they ever so lonely, I find a sweet home . . .
I have storm-worn Castles away on the Rhine;
    In Isles of Greece I have bowers;
I have pilgrim-tents in Palestine,
    On the Nile, old Temple Towers;
And a cedar-palace, a royal one,
    'Neath the snow-covered heights of Lebanon . . .
And what though I love not the bleak Northern
    Isles
    With their murky and frost-bitten air;
Where a loving heart beats, and a rosy lip smiles,
    Is another sweet home, even there!
And I think, with a sigh, I'll abandon the rest
For a home in old England, the last and the best.
Then away with thee, poet, philosopher, fool—
    To the terrible clime of thy birth,
The place where thy boyhood was tortured at
    school,
    The still dearest spot upon earth;
To the green little Isle with the weeping skies
And the girl whom you left with the tears in her
    eyes!

MARRIAGE AND PHOTOGRAPHY

Soon after Frith's return in 1860 from his third tour of the East, he married Mary Ann Rosling, daughter of Alfred and Rachel Rosling, a prominent Reigate Quaker family. Francis was thirty-eight and his bride was twenty-two. Francis Frith was a careful and persistent suitor. 'How anxiously, . . . did I watch for a responsive glance of the eye, or touch of the hand! . . . I took infinite pains, as a man ought to do, to make her love me. I should never have thought of asking for her hand, until I almost knew that she would give it. Men who try to snatch a girl's heart from her, or who "propose" before they have taken any reasonable pains to win, deserve to lose.' The affluent adventurer now wanted to settle with his newly acquired wife and responsibilities.

I reckon the real substance of my life to date from my wedding day. Things that happened before then were more or less of an antediluvian aspect, a preparatory and provisional character, a character of incompleteness—in clear contrast with the subsequent history of mind and spirit. Heretofore, I had not accomplished, nor even attempted anything that professed to be of a lasting or definite character. Now I felt not only that the time had come for serious and steady mental resolves and purposes; but that along with the occasion and the necessity, came also the will and power . . . Possibly 'life in earnest' ought to have begun much earlier. But mental faculties and powers often appear to mature coincidentally with circumstances.

'Life in earnest' meant professional photography.

It seems reasonable to assume that Frith would have become acquainted with professional photographers and their techniques through his early printing business. Frith

Mary Ann Frith

Chatsworth

would have been drawn naturally to this new medium, with its blend of art and science. It provided an incentive to travel, and, for the first time, enabled accurate records of far-distant and romantic places to be brought back. Frith, being a shrewd business man, saw the advantages of combining such photography with his printing establishment. He began by driving his horse and trap around country estates and photographing the homes, mansions and castles of the prosperous middle and upper class Victorian families. This gave him the background of photographic knowledge necessary for his middle-eastern journeys.

On all his Nile expeditions, he worked with three cameras of different sizes: a standard studio camera using glass plates of 8×10ins; a dual lens camera that made side-by-side steroscopic pictures for three-dimensional viewers; and a mahogany monster using glass plates of 16×20ins.

The difficulties involved with such cumber-some equipment can not be exaggerated. Frith not only had to transport these huge cameras by boat, mule, and dromedary (as he called the camels), but also had to take with him a darkroom, as at that time plates had to be prepared and developed immediately. Imagine Frith's caravan crossing a desert with the cameras, fragile glass sheets, chemicals and darkroom equipment carefully packed and strapped to mules. He would see a tomb or monument which he wished to photograph, and all the paraphernalia would be unpacked and the darkroom tent pitched in the desert. The camera would then be set up and the view checked on the ground glass screen, upside down and reversed, under a stifling black cloth.

A photographer only knows—he only can appreciate the difficulty of getting a view satisfactorily into the camera: foregrounds are especially perverse; distance too near or too far; the falling away of the ground; the intervention of some brick wall or other commonplace object, which

Photographic equipment

things (with plenty of others of a similar character) are the rule, not the exception. I have often thought, when manoeuvring about for a position for my camera, of the exclamation of the great mechanist of antiquity: 'Give me a fulcrum for my lever, and I will move the world'. Oh what pictures we would make, if we could command our points of view!

Frith would then enter the light proof, and therefore airless, tent. A glass sheet would be selected and cleaned, and a mixture made of collodion (a solution of pyroxyl in equal parts of alcohol and ether) potassium and other iodides. This viscous liquid, with the consistency of syrup, was then poured onto the glass. Taking care that the liquid was not spilt up his sleeve, Frith would rock the plate until it was evenly coated. It is a tricky manoeuvre in the best of conditions; in a desert tent, it must have been a feat of endurance. Frith reported that the temperature in the tent was often so high (reaching 130°F) that the collodion boiled on hitting the glass. Drops of sweat, flies and sand pitted the surface of the emulsion. The solvents evaporated quickly leaving the collodion adhering to the glass in a smooth, uniform layer. The plate was then dipped into a 'sensitizing' bath of silver nitrate, which deposited a coat of light-sensitive silver salts on the emulsion. It was then loaded into a light-tight holder. The collodion emulsion could not be developed when dry, so Frith had to expose and develop his plate at once. He returned to the camera, checked his screen, inserted the plate holder, withdrew a sheath, uncovering the emulsion inside the camera, and made his exposure.

> I do not prefer to work rapidly upon a landscape, from which I may pass away for ever, but rather slowly; for if you are working with rapid collodion, half a second more or less exposure may spoil your picture. I prefer taking about forty seconds.

Rushing back to the dark tent, Frith developed the plate immediately with gallic or pyrogallic acid. He 'fixed' the image with hypo, or a cyanide salt, which was rinsed out of the emulsion in a bucket of water. And so they packed away the chemicals, dismantled the tent, folded up the camera,

Suez

loaded the mules and set off in search of a fresh view.

Although the wet-plate process was most inconvenient to work, the results were excellent. Failures were few and the speed was adequate for the brilliant light of the desert. The plates have good contrast and excellent definition. It was not until 1871, eleven years after Frith's return from his photographic travels, that an English physician (Richard Leach Maddox) produced the first workable plate which could be prepared weeks or months before exposure and developed at leisure. The photographer needed no longer to take his darkroom on assignment. By 1878 there were four dry-plate makers in Britain, and Frith switched to the more convenient process.

The sheer physical labour involved in this enterprise must be admired. I have a crate of Frith's 16 × 20ins glass plates, made in 1858, and although it contains only a small proportion of his total pictures in this size, it can only be lifted by two men with difficulty. The transportation of many such crates on mules and dromedaries across the country for months on end and the bringing of them safely back to England reveals a little of Frith's tenacity and organisational ability. Helmut Gernsheim, the photographic historian, has said that Frith's 16 × 20ins photographs are the largest of that period which have come to his notice.

When in the desert, Frith wore arab costume. Not only was it more practical than his frock coat, it was also less conspicuous, an important point when travelling amongst wild, and often hostile, groups of natives. The arabs called Frith 'the man who draws pictures on his belly'. When developed, he would show the plates to his companions, in order to gain their interest and co-operation.

Frith was disappointed that the photographic problems hampered the quality of the results.

I think I will confess to a weakness for rapid production in all that I undertake . . . I regret many imperfections, of which I am fully conscious. I regret, especially, that I was so grievously hurried whilst taking my views. Most undoubtedly I might have done more justice to my subjects—yet, when I reflected upon the circumstances under which many of the photographs were taken, I marvel greatly that they turned out so well. Now in a smothering little tent, with my collodion fizzing—boiling up all over the glass the instant that it touched—and, again, pushing my way backwards, upon my hands and knees, into a damp, slimy, rock-tomb, to manipulate—it is truly marvellous that the results should be presentable at all.

Frith experimented with other darkrooms than his suffocating little tent. He tried using the nearby rock tombs for coating and developing his plates, but the dust that permeated the air caused pin-pricks of black on the final print. He erected a darkroom on his boat, which solved the dust menace, but was obviously unsuitable for inland photography. This boat can be seen in the foreground of Frith's photograph 'Hypaethral Temple at Philae'. Frith tried a specially made wicker-work carriage, that he had transported to Egypt from England. This was the most satisfactory solution to the dust, sand, heat and manoeuvrability problems—and it did have the curious and advantageous side-effect of enhancing Frith's prestige among the Arabs:

This carriage of mine, being entirely overspread with a loose cover of white sailcloth to protect it from the sun, was a most conspicuous and mysterious-looking vehicle, and excited amongst the Egyptian populace a vast amount of ingenious speculation as to its uses. The idea, however, which seemed the most reasonable and therefore obtained the most, was that therein, with right laudable and jealous care, I transported from place to place—my harem! It was full of moon-faced beauties, my wives all!—and great was the respect and consideration which this view of the case procured for me.

Even on his return to this country, with his exposed and developed plates, his photographic difficulties were not over. He printed the plates onto paper, coated with the whites of chicken eggs (albumen). This coating held the emulsion on the surface of the paper. Earlier papers without the albumen produced images which were rather dull and degraded, since the image was largely soaked into the paper fibres and not sitting cleanly on the surface. Frith 'sensitized' this paper, in his darkroom, using a similar technique to the plates. He then placed the paper in contact with the plate and exposed the sandwich to daylight for minutes or hours, depending on the brightness of the day, until the image was fixed. As enlargement was unknown, he had to have his glass plates cut to the size required for the final print 16×20ins. Print-making was, for Frith, 'expensive and tedious'. 'I flatter myself that the style of printing which has been employed, is very superior in brilliancy and "tone", and time alone will decide whether it is, as I believe it to be, permanent.' Frith's prints are permanent enough. Unfortunately, he did not know that by mounting the print onto card, he immediately shortened its life expectancy. The glue emits acid fumes which cause the print's image to fade. By comparison, his unmounted prints are beautifully rich in quality.

PRINTS FOR SALE

The newly married Frith now began his 'life in earnest'. He opened a photographic business, F. Frith and Co, in Reigate, Surrey, and began to exploit the results of his photographic expeditions.

His trips to the East had made Frith famous. On his return from his second expedition he walked into a meeting at the Photographic Society in London. He was recognised, and the speaker was informed that 'Mr Frith is in the room'. The chairman was informed, announced his presence and welcomed him back to the society. At the news, the audience 'rapturously' cheered

their distinguished visitor. *The Times* insisted that Frith's photographs 'carry us far beyond anything that is in the power of the most accomplished artist to transfer to his canvas'.

The 16×20in pictures (after cropping, they measure approximately $14\frac{1}{2} \times 19$in) were mounted onto card and three of these views plus their descriptions were issued to subscribers, at 10 shillings each. The complete set of sixty views (dating from 1857), with commentary by a Mrs Poole and Reginald Stuart Poole, was usually bound into a complete book and titled *Cairo, Sinai, Jerusalem and the Pyramids of Egypt*. The smaller camera also yielded enough pictures for a series of publications. Issued monthly in twenty-five parts, at 10 shillings each, they contained three photographic views, size 7×9in. On completion of the subscribers' orders, the remaining prints and letterpress were bound into two volumes and titled *Egypt and Palestine*. This time Francis Frith wrote his own commentary to his pictures, confessing: 'I can only write rapidly, and in the very words which first occur: I dare not revise—out goes one half that I have written, and the remainder is intolerably dull.' Frith's introduction to his book begins with these words:

Were but the character of the Pen for severe truthfulness as unimpeachable as that of the Camera, what graphic pictures might they together paint! . . . I am too deeply enamoured of the georgeous, sunny East, to feign that my insipid, colourless pictures are by any means *just* to her spiritual charms. But, indeed, I hold it to be impossible by any means, fully and truthfully to inform the mind of scenes which are wholly foreign to the eye. There is no effectual substitute for actual travel, but it is my ambition to provide for those to whom circumstances forbid that luxury, *faithful* representations of the scenes I have witnessed, and I shall endeavour to make the simple truthfulness of the Camera a guide for my Pen . . .

The book was wildly successful. The demand for the series continued for many years,

The Great Pyramid, from the Plain

to be greater than he could supply, 'owing to the slowness of the photographic printing'. He made over 2,000 copies of this series, which meant making and mounting over 150,000 prints. Obviously, he could not have carried out this work single-handed; it was done by his employees at Reigate under his supervision.

The stereoscopic camera pictures were also printed in book form: *Egypt, Nubia and Ethiopia*, published by Smith, Elder & Co, London, in 1862. This book contained 100 pairs of prints, together with descriptions and numerous wood engravings by Joseph Bonami FRSL (author of *Nineveh and its Palaces*) and notes by Samuel Sharpe (author of *The History of Egypt*). It seems that Francis Frith was commissioned to take these stereoscopic views before leaving for Egypt on his last trip in 1859. The book says 'The following sun pictures . . . were made for

Messrs Negretti and Zambra by Mr Frith.' A tag inserted in the front of the book reads: 'The stereoscopes specially adapted for use with this volume, compactly folded in an elegant pocket book form, fit for the drawing room table, price 5 shillings and upwards, may be had at Messrs Negretti and Zambra, 1 Hatton Gardens, EC; 59 Cornhill, EC and 122 Regent St. W.'

The stereo viewer was an indispensable amusement in all the best Victorian families. It was the television of the age. The exoticism of Frith's subject matter would have thrilled the Victorians, and made his stereoscopic views extremely popular. The pious Victorians must also have loved Frith's views of the Holy Land, particularly when pasted into the actual pages of the bible. Such a bible, illustrated with photographic views by Francis Frith, appeared in 1862. It was the most expensive of Frith's books; a limited edition of 170 copies, costing 50 guineas each.

Francis Frith made one more volume of pictures from his Eastern travels; a book which poses an intriguing problem. This beautiful little volume contains sixty original prints, which are probably halves of stereo pairs, all of which are captioned in Frith's own handwriting. The book is titled: *In memory of the winter of 1860–61* and dedicated, in Frith's writing, to: 'Rachel Rosling, from F. & M. A. F.' (Francis and Mary Ann Frith). Why the winter of 1860–61? By that time Frith was back in England. What special event took place at that time to urge him to produce a special edition of his Egyptian pictures for Rachel, his mother-in-law? A clue appears in a family bible, in which is inserted a black-edged funeral card: 'In remembrance of William . . . who died on the Nile, near Es Siout in the 14th of 12th month 1860 in the 25th year of his age'. William was Mary Ann's brother. We know that Francis took a companion on his last expedition. Was it William, who stayed in Cairo when Francis returned to England?

OTHER PHOTO-BOOKS

These publications exploiting his travels in the East were not the first, and by no means the last, to appear under the name of Francis Frith. The earliest book containing Frith photographs, that I know of, is *Memorials of Cambridge* a series of views of the Colleges, Halls, Churches and other Public Buildings in the University and Town of Cambridge. This two-volume book was by Charles Henry Cooper FSA who, in his introduction to the 1858 edition wrote: 'By an arrangement with an eminent photographer he [the Proprietor] has been enabled to introduce into this edition views of its University in its present state, executed in the first style of art, which cannot fail to give additional value and to entitle it to a place amongst the first illustrated Works of the Day.' The book contains

sixteen prints, tipped into the pages. If indeed Frith was the author of the pictures, he must have been an 'eminent photographer' before his travels to the East, since we know that he was in Egypt the year before the book was published.

In 1864 Frith published two curious books, written, photographed and published by himself and called *The Gossiping Photographer at Hastings* and *The Gossiping Photographer on the Rhine*. They are both light-hearted, personal, flippant and relatively uninformative travelogues; quaint, but tiresome. The following quotations from the Hastings book will give you a good idea of its literary flavour. It opens with these words:

> Not to use a stronger term, and if it be not wrong—morally and sentimentally wrong—to say so, I dislike the sea. I lately read that some great man, Edward Irving or Achilles—I really forget which—whenever he was in trouble, resorted to the sea shore for comfort; and a comment was added, that 'great minds', when they have discarded every other species of sentimentality, return this habit. It struck me, however, that a fortnight's uninterrupted sea-sickness might perhaps cure them of this remaining weakness.

It is not clear how much these sentiments are an accurate reflection of Frith's own mind and how much they are gossipy fiction. There is an uneasy mixture in the text of informality and facts.

> I saw half-a-dozen 'tars' sitting upon pitch barrels and crab-cradles, knotting tarred rope into nets. Pointing my camera at the features of the place—the net-makers, the cliff, and some of the black boxes—I besought rigidity for a moment. Not only was it cheerfully granted, but when the picture was taken . . . the captain despatched to me a sturdy Ganymede, to whose tarry fingers stuck a huge jug of beer, and, 'Would I drink?' O most noble prince of net-makers and fishermen! never was I so near regretting that I do not drink that vile compound, which is to thee and to they simple-minded mates a sort of elixir of life.

Francis Frith is back in his articulate and honest form in his next book, an illustrated version of Henry W. Longfellow's *Hyperion*, published by Alfred William Bennett, London, in 1865. Frith, accompanied by his wife Mary Ann, travelled along the Rhine, into Switzerland and the Tyrol, in the footsteps of Paul Fleming, the hero of Longfellows' romance. In the 'artist's' preface, Frith wrote:

> The sinular fitness of this beautiful matter-of-fact Romance for Photographic Illustration, was repeatedly felt by the Artist during his long and delightful journey in the footsteps of Paul Fleming . . . And yet—even under the most favourable circumstances—how greatly the rigid inflexibility of the Camera mars the pleasure and the probable success of such an undertaking, no one but the Artist can fully comprehend, therefore . . . he would bespeak the utmost liberality of criticism, especially from those who are not practically acquainted with the artistic difficulties of the work . . .

Francis and Mary Ann spent six weeks on their journey, and twenty-four pictures were eventually used in the book. Frith was much amused that, having taken a photograph of a favourite inn, and presented a print to the owner, it was displayed on the wall bearing the inscription: 'In memory of *Monsieur* Mary Ann Frith from England.'

The Book of the Thames, by Mr and Mrs S. C. Hall, was also illustrated by Frith photographs. It was published in 1867. Another interesting little book illustrated by Frith photographs was *Dovedael*, sold by E. Bamford of Ashbourne. This publication contains ten views of Derbyshire, without an introduction or any description. Each page contains a tipped in print, surrounded by a red border and red printed caption of the subject matter.

DOCUMENTING ENGLAND

After a few years of hard and uphill work, Frith's photographic business at Reigate began to make money. Frith aimed to take photographs of every possible city, town and village in England, Scotland, Wales and Ireland, including famous beauty spots, beach scenes, churches and historic monuments, parks and palaces, country trades, rivers, waterfalls, triumphs of industrialisation, festivals, ceremonies and pageants. The aim was not to sell photographic prints or book illustrations; rather, the original prints were to be used as 'masters' from which postcards could be printed (in Saxony) and sold in their thousands to newsagents, tobacconists and stationers by a team of representatives.

This was a colossal investment in time, energy and money. Frith undoubtedly took most of the early pictures himself but, with the printing and distribution to be organised, was eventually forced to employ assistants who shared the photography. Although it is impossible to state categorically that Frith actually exposed the plate for any particular picture, it is still fair to attribute the results to him. The photographs are undoubtedly stamped with his style and authority so that even his assistants' work is indistinguishable from his own. This is comparable to the photographs of the American Civil War attributed to Mathew Brady. Brady assigned at least twelve different photographers to various battlefields and it is doubtful if Brady himself took even one of the photographs bearing his name. Yet no photographic historian would quibble with the fact that they are, in essence, Mathew Brady pictures.

Francis Frith and his assistants would arrive by train and then hire a horse and trap 'systematically' to cover the assigned shooting area. There was no rush; they would wait four hours for an exposure in a cathedral interior, four days for the right light on a view. Most of these early pictures were taken on 8×12in glass plates; later changed to 8×6in format. The materials for a prolonged shooting assignment, the heavy mohogany camera capable of exposing these large plates, with a wooden tripod and all the other necessary accessories, made such photographic trips a physical endurance course. Without the heat, flies and darkroom tent of the desert, it still was not a matter of jumping into a car with a Leica and a pocketful of film.

As well as his bulky photographic gear, Francis Frith usually took with him, even on his European travels, his entire household—wife, children, nursemaid, coachman. Frith pictures usually feature one of the family or servants acting as a point of interest and indication of scale—always subservient to the view.

Francis Frith & Co was not only the first photographic publishing firm in Britain, it rapidly became the largest in the world. This demand for quantity inevitably led to a decline in quality. Frith himself was, indirectly, to write an indictment of his later work in a comment addressed to other photographers.

> The rapidity of production of which the merely mechanical process of photographic picture-making is capable, may easily become a source of great mischief. The student should bear in mind that what he has to aim at is not the production of a large number of *good* pictures but if possible, of *one* that shall satisfy all the requirements of his judgement and taste. That one when produced will be, we need not say, of infinitely greater value to his feelings and reputation than a lane-full of merely good pictures.

In its heyday, the Reigate factory housed a bewildering array of photographic services. The stock of unmounted photographs alone exceeded one million prints, with pictures from Britain, Germany, Austria, Switzerland, Italy, Spain, Portugal, Norway, France, Egypt, Palestine, America, Algeria, China, Japan and India. His postcards were on sale in over 2,000 shops in England. He supplied photographs for artists and architects; developed, retouched and printed amateur's pictures and even gave them lessons in photography. He supplied to order opalines, frames, medallions and morocco leather albums. He offered sets of lantern slides, calendars, Christmas, birthday or souvenir cards. And he still offered 'Advantageous terms for taking photographs of groups, estates, private residences, etc.' Frith & Co even dabbled in news photography, and achieved a scoop by taking the photograph of a suffragette committing suicide by throwing herself beneath King Edward's horse at the Derby. The early prosperity of Francis Frith & Co left him free to devote more and more of his time to his family and leisure involvements.

FAMILY LIFE

'A man ought to wash his hands and perfume his lips before he writes or speaks about these

Mary Ann Frith

Brightlands

things: very gracious and tender ought the words to be!' There is no doubt that Francis Frith had an idyllic marriage. He had 'the best gift in life, a loving and true woman's heart.'

Mary Ann was a daughter of another Quaker family, the Roslings, of Reigate, who were active in the timber importing trade, dealing especially with Norway. She and Francis lived for a time in a house named Churchfell, not far from Reigate Parish Church, conveniently close to the Friends' Meeting House. They later moved to a large rambling house, Brightlands, also in Reigate. It was an ideal place for raising a family— no near neighbours, plenty of lawns and trees, and room enough for many children. The lawn was so large that it had to be mowed by a machine and pony, wearing leather shoes to prevent damage to the turf. Mary Ann kept a diary of the Brightland days, of their picnics, and travels into the countryside; it was a prosaic, personal diary, its entries were merely memory-joggers— 'Frank made a lot of good pictures and enjoyed having the family about him', 'Had a picnic. Frank lit the stove, boiled our eggs and made the tea.' Not great literature, but the pages exude a cosy warmth about their relationship. Francis was often invited to attend Quaker meetings throughout the country, particularly in the north of England. Whenever possible, Mary Ann accompanied him. They would be entertained at the homes of Friends for a day or two, and Francis would take the opportunity of driving out into the countryside, adding to his stock of photographic views. In his most prosperous period, he had built a large house on the Downs overlooking the Weald—but they never had enough time or money to inhabit it.

Francis and Mary Ann had eight children: five sons, Eustace, Francis Edgar, Cyril,

(above) *Brightlands*; (below) *Francis Frith and family*

Julius and Clement, who died in infancy; and three daughters, Alice, Mabel and Susan. They were a close-knit and affectionate family, surrounded by solid, but never ostentatious, Victorian comfort. The house was filled with the odour of cedar-wood, from the drawing room, and turpentine and fresh-painted canvases from Francis' work-room. Hanging in the hall were the antelope horns, bagged after his dromedary chase in the desert above the Sixth Cataract of the Nile. Other spoils from his travels dotted the house, including treasures from China which had reputedly found their way to Reigate via Africa from the sack of Peking.

The children were brought up in the Quaker tradition of a quiet religious home, which was never sanctimonious or over strict. When not at school or having lessons from a governess, they often roamed the North Down hills above Reigate, engaged in nature study, botany, fossil collecting, etc. Break-fast conversation would be sprinkled with 'thee' and 'thou'. After the meal, Francis would read a short passage from the bible, which would be followed by a few moments of silence. It is unlikely that Frith indulged in the Victorian ritual of family prayers, for no Friend would preach or offer a spoken prayer unless spontaneously 'moved by the spirit'. At one Quaker funeral attended by Frith, an elder was asked to say a few words. The reply was 'I don't keep prayer on tap'. In this spirit, the Frith household was spiritual but not sactimonious, pious but not prejudiced.

Francis was a conservative dresser in black frock coat, grey waistcoat, white shirt and bowtie. Outside he would wear a French silk hat (a low-crowned grey felt one, in the summer) and cover his shoulders with a cape when the weather became chilly or wet. The only sartorial gesture against conformity was Frith's magnificent beard and long hair. Enthusiasm for the Crimean war had led to short back-and-sides, and only 'arty types'

Francis Frith

kept their long locks. The illustration above shows Francis Frith in a beautiful silk oriental jacket, reclining on a couch during one of his trips to the East. This jacket is still in the Frith family, and would indicate that he was about 5ft 9in tall and of slim build, certainly no more than 38in round the chest.

FRITH FAMILY BALLADS
When Francis arrived home in the evening, dinner would be served and then the family would gather by the fireside for home amusements. The Frith family would read aloud from the works of Tennyson, Carlyle, Browning, Longfellow and, of course, Shake-speare. Mary Ann would sit quietly with her crochet, while Francis would sketch a little, paint in oils, plan his addresses to the Quaker meetings, write poems, and make up verses for the amusement of the children.

33

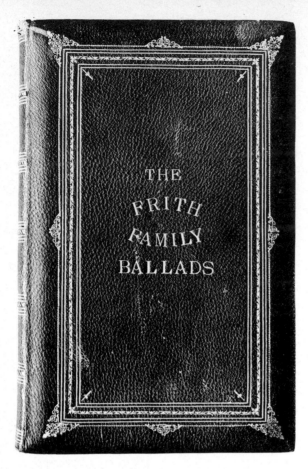

Frith Family Ballads

These verses were written down—in a beautiful handscript, the titles embellished with intricate designs and even photographs—in *The Frith Family Ballads*, a leather-bound book, which still remains in the family. A typical verse from this ballad book is:

Ode to a Shrimp

Oh Shrimp! whose home is the water blue
  I often and longingly think of you
As you sport in the grotto and coral cave
  For life must have charms 'neath the ocean
    wave.
It's all very well, the Shrimp replied
  To be cradled to rest by the flowing tide,
To be waked by the Seagull's low sad cry,
  And be fanned by the breezes sweeping by,
It's all very well to have plenty of fun
  With the mermaids at play when their work is
    done,
To watch the Sun set under glowing skies,

And to dance with glee when the billows rise.
But, the fisher-boy sings in his boat on the bay
  As he catches shrimps all the livelong day,
And his sister shouts with a fiendish glee
  As she eats those shrimps at her early tea!
For devoured alike by rich and by poor,
  A shrimp's life is short, and his death is sure!

There were the continental trips to break the monotony of these winter evenings. The huge travelling coach, loaded down with family, servants, luggage, photographic and painting equipment would set off for the Rhine, Austria, the South of France or Italy. On one trip, when Eustace was about three years old he escaped from his nurse who was bathing him, and rushed onto the balcony of the German hotel, stark naked. Mary Ann, the demure Victorian girl, was horrified. Francis was secretly amused, and passed the story down to his grandchildren.

CHILDREN AND GRANDCHILDREN

Later in his life, when the business was prospering and occupying little of his time, and his children married with families of their own, Francis and Mary Ann moved away from Reigate to Mooredge, a delightful house looking out across Walton Heath, at that time completely unspoiled and undeveloped. This was Frith's summer home until his death. The grandchildren would often stay there and remembered Francis' kindness. One of them recalled that 'my grandfather made us a kite. He was fond of interesting the children in this way. Once constructed he took us out to the Heath to show us how to fly it. It went up beautifully. But while running backwards, looking up at the kite, he tripped and fell headlong. There was great excitement among the children because normally he was so dignified, and this kind of behaviour was so unlike him. His grey felt hat rolled off into the bushes and it was our task to recover it.'

Francis' health was never very robust and he suffered in the winter from bronchitis and asthma. During the last twenty years of his life, he was obliged to winter abroad, either at Cannes or San Remo. Often one of their grandchildren would join them.

The greatest tragedy that befell, the otherwise extremely happy, Frith family was the early death, by drowning, of their son Francis Edgar, while on a schoolboy holiday in Norway. In April 1872, Frith had written, to another of his sons, a strangely prophetic poem, which opens:

Dear boy, of Saxon linneage and name,
When eight eventful years go, the light
Of this dim island in the Northern Seas,
Bad welcome! while another gush welled up
From that unfailing source, a Mother's love;
And yet another cord of strong, sweet care
Wound round a Father's heart,—
    Dear Son of Mine!
I greet thee with an eight year's love, new born,
But vigorous with promise of a life
Old as the ages of Eternity!
Which of us first, the Father or the Son,
Shall cross the bound-line where an earthborn
    love
Grows to the measure of a Seraph's Soul?
I know not: for a sudden strain may snap
The strongest cable, let the stateliest ship
Drift to the unknown, infinite expanse,
Whilst petty anchored barks, wave turned old,
More gently handled may live out the gale.
If first thou fall into the cold embrace,
May no dark shadow of an ill-spent day,
No strain of childish, unrepented sin
Mar the air-meeting of thy dear young soul
With Him who gave it, and who died to save!...

It would be possible to fill this book with Frith's poems. Some are nonsense verses for the amusement of his children and grandchildren; others are absurd ballads which recount legends and tales of the East. Scores of these were written in Egypt and were undoubtedly used to enliven lectures delivered on his return; others are introverted and personal, among which my favourite is *My Overcoat*, about his old fly-fishing coat, patched and darned, stained and torn, but cherished; yet others are deep spiritual and philosophical explorations, like *The Autobiography of a Soul*.

His religious works were not restricted to poetry; he wrote several books about Quakerism. His prose is clear, crackling and boils with barely concealed rhetoric:

There is, in truth, a great persistent rotteness at the root of the matter in society at large! There are *very few* people who will break with old habits and associations, for the sake of conforming their religious profession and practice to their convictions, *unless it improves, at the same time their social position*!... One can hardly avoid thinking, and sometimes speaking, of the moral flabbiness —this worldliness and irreligious cowardice— with pity, and even with a degree of contempt.

In 1877, he published a twenty-eight page booklet costing 6d explaining in lucid and persuasive prose the doctrine of *Evangelica-*

'Ode to a Shrimp' from the Frith Family Ballads

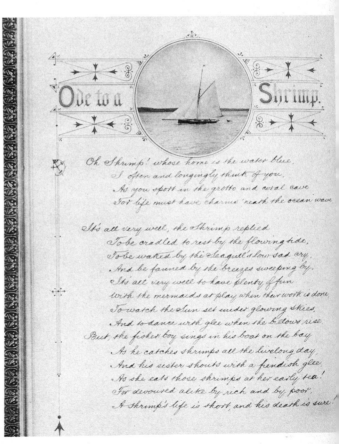

lism from the standpoint of the Society of Friends. *The Quaker Ideal*, published in 1893, was a much more ambitious work of 102 pages. His purpose was 'not to write history, but rather to present an ideal picture of what I conceive nineteenth-century Quakerism ought to be, and to some extent actually is.' In Frith's opinion, a fair and truthful history of the Society had not yet been written. It needed an author of special background and with intimate knowledge of the subject.

> Only a Quaker scholar, 'to the manner born', perhaps with some generations of Quaker blood in his veins, a man of large sympathies, and possessing an intimate knowledge of the entire subject could hope to do it any sort of justice . . . No, the task is impossible to an outside observer. You might as well introduce an uneducated rustic

to the Apollo Belvedere or the Discobolus, and expect him to be awed by their artistic beauty. Probably all that he would notice would be the pecularity of their costume. For, indeed, the public has become used to judge of us almost exclusively by such 'outward and visible signs' as dress and language, and the legend of inviolable silence which has fastened upon us . . .

In other words, the Quaker history should be written by a man like Francis Frith. If that sounds like a snide remark, note that only a couple of pages earlier, Frith had written:

> the writer may fairly claim to have had large opportunity for the study of his subject, having been for nearly half-a-century a close observer of all that relates to the Society, a diligent reader of its literature, and during the greater part of that time a deeply interested participator in its affairs . . . I was the son of out-and-out Quaker parents.

RETIREMENT AND DEATH

Francis Frith's later years were spent in the enviable manner of a gentleman of leisure, reverting to the days of idleness of his youth: 'I fell back upon books and art, nature love and poetry.' His business had prospered. 'After some years of hard and uphill work, it became remunerative, and has been a source of pleasure and profit, with very few drawbacks, ever since. I am hurrying on to have done with business, once for all. It now (in my sixty-third year) occupies very little of my attention.' What did occupy his attention was his family and his photography, his spiritual writings and the affairs of the Society of Friends, his poetry and his paintings. Frith's oil paintings were landscapes of the countryside, mostly done on holiday. He loved the Lake District, which he often visited with Mary Ann, stopping off to fish the Derbyshire streams of his boyhood. Many of the paintings depict the scenery of the South of France or Italy, and were created on his winters abroad, during the later years of his life.

He was often accompanied on his painting excursions by his close friend, J. B. Surgey. They did not seem to take their art particularly seriously, often contributing to each others canvases. Frith, certainly, never exhibited his paintings or even signed them. Dozens of these quiet, passive landscapes still exist, and adorn the walls of the homes of Frith's grandsons. They are typical of the academic style of realism beloved by the amateur Victorian artist. This is not to say that they are bad paintings—Frith was obviously an extremely accomplished craftsman in oils—but they are interchangeable with the work of many painters of similar standing in the period. As painters struggled for the realism of the camera, the photographers of the period chased Art, even if this meant rejecting the intrinsic characteristics that made their medium unique. Oily daubs, scratched plates, soft focus, tints and toners were all used to give the appearance of a (bad) salon painting. In fact, it was the non-photographers of this period who have left us the richest heritage.

Oil painting by Francis Frith

Oil painting by Francis Frith

By 'non-photographers' I mean those men who were not *primarly* concerned with creating artistic images, but used the camera as a means of communicating discoveries and interests in other, non-aesthetic fields. The best Victorian photographers were social campaigners, Fleet Street men, explorers and travellers—like Francis Frith. His paintings are also 'photographic' in the sense that his choice of viewpoint and the precision of his detail and perspective are consistent with the photographs that he made of similar scenes. Black and white reproductions of his paintings are remarkably similar to photographs. But perhaps the end result was less important than the act of painting. In the South of France, in the open air, he could paint and think and relax. It on one of these winter holidays that he died.

He was buried in a plot, now owned by the Frith family, in the Protestant Cemetery at Cannes, early in 1898. He was seventy-six years old. *The Photographic News* of 18 March, 1898 ran the following sparse, eight line obituary:

> The death has occurred at Cannes of Mr Francis Frith, an old and prominent member of the Society of Friends. The deceased gentleman, who was in his seventy-sixth year, was formerly head of the well-known firm of Messrs Frith & Co, photographers, and while actively engaged in artistic pursuits he gained many distinctions, including that of being the first person to take a camera up the Nile, where he used it to great purpose.

Soon after the funeral Mary Ann returned to Mooredge with her unmarried daughter Mabel, who had spent the winter with them in Cannes. They decided that they did not want to stay on there and the summer was spent in arranging for certain pieces of furniture, pictures and family possessions to go to the homes of her children, and for the sale of the house in the autumn. She and Mabel then spent one more winter at the rented villa in Cannes, before going to live with Eustace and his family at St Ippolits at Reigate Hill, where Mary Ann remained until her death, and Mabel until her marriage a year or two later.

FRANCIS FRITH & CO

At Frith's death, the company was already in the care of his sons Eustace and Cyril. It was Eustace's idea that instead of farming out the printing of the postcards to Saxony, Francis Frith & Co should start its own printing works, under the management of Cyril. The experiment was not very successfully, for two reasons. The location of the works was Charlfield in Gloucestershire, which was remote and a difficult journey, in those days, from the Reigate establishment. Also, not enough was known about the highly skilled process of collotype printing. This process was invented in 1855, but not commercially viable until 1868. It is ideal for reproducing delicate detail especially fassimile reproductions of paintings in monochrome, and for short runs. The results are clear with little grain structure, since no screen is used. It admirably suited the production of postcards, but it was a craft that needed the skill and knowledge of the German printers. In fact, when the Charlfield experiment failed, the printing was sent back to Saxony, Cyril having died some years previously, around 1911.

The printing business was sold, or almost given away, to three of the staff who bravely continued with inadequate capital, throughout World War I, when they nearly collapsed. After the war, the company was joined by Frith's grandson—Francis E. Frith. The Cotswold Collotype Company, as it was later called, had moved to the pretty country town of Wotton-under-Edge in 1909, and

Francis Frith's burial certificate

under Francis E. Frith's leadership, its skills improved tremendously and the business prospered. Not only did it win back the printing of all the F. F. & Co postcards, but they also did collotype printing for all the major postcard publishers. Francis E. Frith, now retired, still lives in Wotton-under-Edge.

Meanwhile the photographic company at Reigate was also prospering, under the control of Eustace Frith and his co-director A. W. Wickman, who had been appointed after Cyril Frith's death. Although the Victorian hobby of collecting new post-cards had declined, demand grew through the

(above) *Wotton-under-Edge, Church St*
(below) *Cravenhurst, Raglan Road, Reigate*

1930s, due to the increasing affluence and greater number of visitors to holiday resorts. However, F. F. & Co began to run into trouble through printing huge quantities of stock, which quickly went out of date and was thus rejected by retailers. Tons of obsolete cards had to be thrown away. Also, competition was fierce, leading to very narrow profit margins. One Frith representative, staying at a hotel in Cornwall in the 1930s reported that five other postcard reps were in competition in the town.

The stock rooms were built around a huge covered court-yard, in which the grandchildren loved to play. The Reigate factory also contained stables, originally used to house the ponies and traps, but later converted into photographic processing rooms. Without the need for millions of spare postcards, the huge works was redundant and was sold to a jam-making firm. The business was transferred to a fine old mansion, Cravenhurst, in Raglan Road, Reigate. This was much more compact, and the keeping of stock was abandoned altogether. New photographs were taken as early as possible in the spring and summer, the orders booked for shops, and delivery made in time for the holiday rush season in August and September.

This demand for a rapid turnover of new pictures was not only an economic trimming of assets, it was also a reflection of the sudden acceleration of the pace of everyday life. In the 1860s Francis Frith could have taken a village scene, confident that it would remain basically unchanged, for scores of years. But this 'period of relevancy' was shrinking, until the need came for a once-yearly turnover.

When Eustace Frith died, his fellow director did not want to continue alone. So A. F. Sargent, who had been in charge of Raphael Tuck Postcard Department, joined Francis Frith & Co as managing director. Directly after the war Mr Sargent was joined in the business by his two sons, Frederick and Trevor, who in turn became managing directors of the company on their father's death in 1959. The sons were energetic and well qualified technically for the job. They rapidly pulled the business together and yet again, it became a tremendous success—until the time came for them to retire. Neither of them had sons who could follow them into the business, and they sold the company in 1968. That was really the end of Francis Frith's work. Pandora, the new owners, concentrated on pretty calendars and twee postcards. The business was bought for a daughter, anxious to run her own company but photographic publishing had become a highly skilled concern. Her lack of experience caused the business to collapse. Francis Frith & Co was placed in liquidation.

Francis E. Frith

River Scenes

KENDAL, HAWES BRIDGE

Francis Frith was a keen amateur artist in oils, although he never exhibited or even signed the results. His painting companion was often his close friend J. B. Surgey, perhaps the figure in this photograph.

PANGBOURNE BRIDGE

This is typical of the type of picture which Frith would convert into a postcard, print in its thousands and sell to newsagents, sweet shops and tobacconists in the neighbouring villages. Very quickly, Francis Frith and Co Ltd, became the largest photographic publishers in the world.

MAIDENHEAD, BOULTERS LOCK

Boulters Lock is the 'entrance' to what is perhaps the most beautiful stretch of the river Thames, Cliveden reach. Small craft must now pass through the lock and cannot bypass it by means of the slipway seen on the left hand side of the picture. However the scene remains much the same today except that the sluice gates are electrically powered rather than being operated by hand.

MAPLEDURHAM MILL

The stagnant mill water is being loaded into the barrel on the back of the cart. This would have been a regular feature of the long summer months when the estate cattle and sheep grazed on the dry hill pastures. In about 1910 a turbine was installed on the left channel. The featureless skies in most of Frith's photographs were due to the fact that emulsions at that time were only sensitive to blue light, and not to the whole range of the visible spectrum as are today's panchromatic films. A few photographers of the period were adept at printing in the skies, made on a separate plate with a shorter exposure time. This slow, complex technique might have suited 'art' photographers, producing a small number of carefully made exhibition prints, but Frith had a commercial eye on quantity.

RIVER DART, DEVON

In the background is Sharpham House, thought to have been designed by Sir Robert Taylor in 1770. The gardens are attributed to Capability Brown. This is a picture of classic composition. Frith was always anxious to include figures in his landscapes, both as a focal point and to give scale to the subject. Thousands of these photographs depict Mary Ann, his wife, who accompanied him on most of his picture-hunting expeditions.

46

ILKLEY STEPPING STONES
Another example where the absence of the figures would have led to a 'flat', lifeless photograph. No doubt, his wife, coachmen and passing farmers and ramblers have been persuaded to contribute to the picture.

NORFOLK BROADS
Since filters were impractical on the colour-blind emulsions of Frith's day, one method of incorporating sky tone without recourse to double exposures or montage was to shoot into the light.

EVESHAM, HAMPTON FERRY

Hampton has long been a ferry point, records going back to the days of the Abbots of
Evesham. Hampton Ferry House, shown in the picture is part of the old established Rudge
estate, and with the lease of the house goes the obligation of running the ferry. It is still in
regular use, the fare for adults is $1\frac{1}{2}$p, $\frac{1}{2}$p for schoolchildren. Many of the photographs in this
book were not taken by Francis Frith. It would have been impossible for one man to have
amassed such a vast collection single-handed. We know that one of his first assistants was
J. Powell, but Frith's style so permeates every picture that it is impossible to differentiate
Frith's work from that of his helpers.

NORWICH, PULLS FERRY

Pulls ferry is named after John Pull, ferryman for forty years until his death in 1841. He was also the keeper of a public house in the cottage shown in the picture. The ferry itself dates back to Elizabethan times. A small fare was charged and the service continued until 1943 when it became uneconomic. The Medieval gateway, on the right, once crossed a canal that transported heavy goods, and possibly even the stones of the Cathedral itself, into the Close. All the reproductions in this book are taken direct from Frith's original albumen prints. Albumen paper was the most widespread method of printing from the second half of the 1850s until around 1890. It was introduced in May 1850 by Blanquart-Evrard, and by 1866 it was estimated that six million whites of egg were used annually in Britain to provide the albumen for photographic paper.

OXFORD FERRY, MARSTON MESOPOTAMIA

The Marston ferry, which is still in operation, carries fare-paying passengers across the river Cherwell between Summertown and Old Marston. Albumen paper was a printing-out process. This meant that the paper was exposed behind the plate until an image appeared which was then fixed. There was no developing. Frith's prints were made in a glass covered shed like a vast greenhouse. The exposure times varied considerably according to the weather but since the paper/plate sandwich was in a frame, a hinged lid on the base allowed the printer to peel back a corner of the paper to check on the progress of the image.

BRAY

A quiet scene of children fishing in the Thames. The landing stage belonged to the George Hotel, now known as the Waterside Inn. The popularity of albumen paper may be gauged by the fact that one company, the Dresden Albuminising Company, used 60,000 chicken eggs per day. Girls were employed solely to break eggs and separate the whites from the yolks. Most albumen paper was made at the time of the year when eggs were cheapest.

RICHMOND BRIDGE

Up until the end of nineteenth century Thames barges carried heavy goods up the river. When Frith first began his photography and throughout the 1860s, which included his Egyptian travels, the photographer in the field used the wet-plate process. This meant that along with his vast camera and tripod, he also needed to transport a dark tent, a box of glass plates, chemicals, dishes, measures and often a supply of water. By the time this photograph was taken, however, dry plates had been introduced which made it possible for a photographer to leave behind the darkroom and process his plates on returning from his travels.

UNKNOWN

The notice *Flussbad* (river bathing establishment) visible beyond the bridge indicates the scene is Germany.

It was not possible for photographers to sneak pictures; candid cameras were unknown. The bulky equipment and elaborate ritual of picture-making made the photographer all-too conspicuous. Also, cameras were a comparative rarity. In the year that Frith began his photography (1850) only fifty-one photographers were registered in the whole of England, according to the census returns of that year. A decade later when he returned from Egypt the number had risen to 2,534.

The Countryside

HAILSHAM, FROM THE SOUTH

It was not only Mary Ann who was pressed into service in Francis's photographs; his children, their nurse and even the coachman were included, not as personalities, merely as ciphers. But once included their place in the picture was not guaranteed for posterity. As fashions changed, albeit at a much slower pace than today, the picture became dated, and hence unsuitable for issue as a postcard. Often on the backs of Frith's portraits are his instructions: 'remove figure'. His retouchers would then paint out the offending person and paint in the background scene. This was carried out with such skill that it is impossible to detect on the final printed postcard.

48482. Hailsham; from South. F.F&Cº.

MERROW

Frith's records of life and landscapes in the nineteenth century were not only very successful (one old but undated catalogue boasts: 'the stock of unmounted photographs on our shelves at Reigate exceeds ONE MILLION prints') but are also extremely valuable today—both for their aesthetic interest and also as aids to the historian. Farriers are a good case in point. Very few remain, and none with such an ornate or appropriate forge entrance.

MILFORD RAILWAY STATION

Time seemed of little account to the Frith photographers. They would wait for days if necessary for the right weather and time of day. They knew that once the best possible picture had been taken it would continue to be relevant, and to sell, for many years to come. After World War I the pace of life quickened so much that this dedicated pursuit of the best had to be subservient to the economics of the company. So many postcard companies were now competing, and price slashing led to unhealthily low margins of profit. The tempo of life was also increasing at an ever-accelerating rate. Whereas once a photograph could be used for twenty years, now new pictures had to be taken annually, the photographer doubling up as representative and postcard seller.

COMPTON, THE SMITHY
The risk that the subject would move was always high when using slow plates. Instantaneous exposures were not possible when Frith first began his photographic business. The head of the smith in this picture is a featureless blur.

MILL AT AGWEN FALLS
The length of Frith's exposure can be judged from the smooth continuity of the water. During a discussion at the Photographic Society in 1858, Frith remarked: 'I do not prefer to work rapidly upon a landscape, from which I may pass away for ever, but rather slowly; for if you are working with rapid collodion, half a second more or less exposure may spoil your picture. I prefer taking about forty seconds'. Most photographers today prefer taking about 1/250 sec or faster.

EVERSLEY, A VILLAGE FRIEND
The knife-grinder would push his cart around the village, stopping outside the door of any home where there were knives, shears or blades to sharpen. The grinding stone was turned by a large (pedal powered) wheel. This is one of the relatively few 'portraits' taken by Frith, although the personality of the sitter is obviously of secondary interest to his photogenic trade.

HINDHEAD, OLD BROOM SQUIRE'S COTTAGE

Like all Victorian photographers, Francis Frith was concerned about the permanency of his pictures. With some justification. Albumen prints were known to have a relatively short life before the richness of their tones softened and flattened. A good deal of work was done between 1850 and 1885 towards finding a permanent print process. One of the most popular was the carbon print invented by Sir Joseph Wilson Swan. Although a few carbon prints by Frith still exist, he was obviously not enthusiastic about the process. In the *Photographic Journal* of 5 March 1859 it is recorded 'Mr Frith had tried the carbon printing, as had several of his friends, and they had all given it up as comparatively hopeless for general purposes.'

CLIFTON HAMPTON, THE BARLEY MOW INN

Most of Frith's albumen prints have remained 'full-bodied' in quality as a side product of the quantity of pictures he produced, rather than as a result of better emulsions or a more refined technique. The secret is that he did not mount the prints onto card (except for his portfolios) but kept them loosely stacked together in boxes. Although he was unaware of the fact, it is often the glue in the card on which prints are mounted that causes the image to fade. His unmounted prints, stored out of the light, still retain their original richness.

EAST KENT HOP PICKERS

In spite of Frith's passionate devotion to Quakerism, he does not seem to have used his camera as a social weapon. When he focuses it on the poor or underprivileged there is always an element of voyeurism, or an acceptance of the class structure as an unalterable fact of life. There is no emotional involvement such as is all too evident in the pictures of the East End poor by Frith's contemporary, John Thompson.

UNKNOWN

On the rare occasions when Frith was tempted to photograph such a character, it is extremely doubtful whether the result was issued as a postcard. It was merely an interesting diversion from his business activities.

OTTERTON, DEVON, HONITON LACE WORKER (MRS FREEMAN)
Honiton was long one of the centres of lacemaking in England; Queen Victoria's wedding dress was of Honiton lace. Though the craft was eclipsed by the arrival of machine lace, it is still taught and practised in the town. Although Frith is reported to have made three separate fortunes during his lifetime, he had a remarkable distaste for business: '. . . the spirit in which money-earning work is done is very often and very largely a cursing spirit . . . that it does complete the moral and even the intellectual degradation of thousands, no thoughtful person can doubt. There is nothing even in commercial success that any man need be proud of'.

WELSH COSTUMES

Francis Frith's best pictures are his landscapes; he seems ill at ease when his camera is confronted by people. He undoubtedly had a remarkable ability for composing his photographs but all too often 'that which here demands homage being chiefly the inflexible severity of truth', as one critic wrote at the time.

PENSARN, WELSH COSTUME

Here again the lengthy exposure time is indicated by the ethereal rendering of the table cloth and plant leaves. Photography's special role in documenting changes in appearance and habit was underlined by Russell's remark that should some historian in Japan (then as remote as the moon) study the characteristics of 'English ladies at two not remote epochs, as represented, say, by Frith (the painter) and by Du Maurier, he would be driven to the conclusion that there had been a complete change of type, due to the introduction of some foreign race . . . from such errors as this we shall be saved by Photography.'

40655.F.F&Co.

LAKESIDE
Cover the figures and it is immediately apparent how much the picture relies on their presence. Frith wrote: 'Very rarely indeed does a landscape arrange itself upon his focusing glass as well, as effectively, as he would arrange it *if he could*'.

TAUNTON, VIVARY PARK, FEEDING PIGEONS

One of the mysteries of photography on its introduction in 1839 was that a group of people did not require a longer exposure than a single portrait. Although the notion seems quaint, it is understandable if the only means of recording at your disposal was a pencil. The first book containing photographs to be published was *The Pencil of Nature* by W. H. Fox Talbot (1844-6). His comment alongside one of his own photographs is equally applicable to Frith's: 'Groups of figures take no longer to obtain than single figures would require . . . but at present we cannot succeed in this art without previous concert and arrangement . . . but when a group of Persons has been artistically arranged, and trained by little practice to maintain an absolute immobility for a few seconds of time, very delightful pictures are easily obtained'.

RUAN MINOR, LIZARD PENINSULA

Frith and his assistant usually travelled by train to the most convenient town near their chosen shooting location. They would then hire a pony and trap in which to load all the cumbersome photographic gear and transport it around the countryside looking for pictures. Opposite the Ruan Minor village school is the forge with the smith in the doorway. The house in the centre distance is the village shop, post office and bakery. It was here that the traditional saffron cakes and splits were made for the village. It was said to be the first place in the area where cakes could be bought and even neighbouring villages ordered supplies from Mitchell's on their feast days.

COOKHAM MOOR, BERKSHIRE

Although gypsies with their hurdy-gurdies are seldom seen on the Moor today, it does have travelling summer fairs each year. This scene is much the same as it was over eighty years ago—except that the road is no longer a dirt track. This picture was taken at the height of Frith's career. His later pictures often sacrifice style for content. In a paper on *The Art of Photography* (1859) Frith wrote, albeit unwittingly, the most objective criticism of his own later photographs: 'The rapidity of production of which the merely mechanical process of photographic picture-making is capable may easily become a source of great mischief. The student should bear in mind that what he has to aim at is not the production of a large number of *good* pictures, but, if possible, of *one* that shall satisfy all the requirements of his judgement and taste'.

BISHAM, BERKSHIRE

Occasionally, if accidentally, a Frith photograph is transformed into a work of art—not owing to the ability with which he handled the content, but by the prosaic job of retouching the print. Leaves are stippled in, highlights cleaned, shadows deepened, edges sharpened—until the result is an exquisite painting. The fact that all this effort and application was purely functional makes it much less pretentious, so much more beautiful.

GODALMING, SURREY MILL LANE

Most of the original glass plates from which these prints were made still exist, but not all.
Many were smashed. Others were given to a major museum—and have not been seen since.
Thousands more were dumped in the garden to make a solid glass wall, 10yds long. Those
that do remain are in remarkably good condition. The emulsions were usually lacquered to
improve their keeping qualities; less effective methods attempted by photographers of the
period included dunking the plates in solutions of tea, coffee, syrup and even beer.

Townscapes

WEYMOUTH, NEW KURSAAL

Kursaal was a word adopted from the German spas and watering places, though in England it lost its curative meaning. The octagonal building provided a convenient shelter for the— here rather sparse—audiences attending the concerts of light music which around the turn of the century very often featured German bands. The straw hat, worn by the park keeper, was a universal summer headgear from the 1890s to World War I. Its postwar eclipse is strange and inexplicable.

LAUNCESTON, MARKET PLACE

One of the most drastic widespread change in sartorial habits over the last eighty years has been the disappearance of the hat. It is rare indeed to find any male, man or boy, in a Frith photograph whose head is not covered, whether by bowler, top-hat, French silk hat, cloth cap or boater. This is true irrespective of class. Even these farmers are wearing bowlers or toppers to a man.

SHREWSBURY, CATTLE MARKET

Shrewsbury is still the thriving capital of agricultural Shropshire. The cattle market is no longer in the centre of the town but has been moved to new premises on the outskirts of Shrewsbury.

PETERSFIELD, HAMPSHIRE, MARKET DAY

The market square is presided over by a king on horseback—but the square is associated with a much more interesting notability, John Small. He was a famous cricketer, an original member of the first cricket club at Hambledon. His linen draper's shop in the square bore the following crude but informative poem:

The Said John Small
Wishes it to be known to all
That he doth make both bat and ball
And will play any man in England
For five pounds a side.

IPSWICH, THE BUTTERMARKET, THE ANCIENT HOUSE
The fifteenth-century house with its projecting upper floor and heavily moulded seventeenth-century ceilings, carved timber and sculpted figures is, as one travel writer remarked, 'an unparalleled extravaganza'. In 1841 the population of Ipswich was about 25,000; today it is four times that number.

CHESTER, THE LECHE HOUSE, WATERGATE STREET
A sixteenth century building with seventeenth century additions. The first floor still forms part of Watergate Row along which it is possible to walk. At one time the house was the property of the Leches of Mollington, who were descended from John Leche, surgeon or leech to Edward III.

PENZANCE

Penzance was prosperous even in the sixteenth century, in spite of its isolation from the rest of Britain. As late as the 1750s a writer complained: 'there was only one cart in the town of Penzance, and if a carriage occasionally appeared in the streets it attracted universal attention'. It was pillaged by the Spaniards in 1595, completely sacked during the Civil War and well into the eighteenth century was subject to pirate attacks from Turkey, Algeria and France. St Mary's Parish Church, seen in Frith's photograph, was built in 1834 of granite ashlar and commands a fine panorama of the bay and surrounding countryside. *Pen-sans* means the 'holy head'.

READING, BROAD STREET

Berkshire was, and to some extent still is, an agricultural county, with Reading as its commercial centre. But the decline of the waterways and the developments of road transport have profoundly affected the appearance of the town. Perhaps the most significant change was caused by the opening of the railway line from London to Reading in 1840. Thousands flocked to see the first train arrive. The journey took 1hr 5 mins—which is a fair time considering that express trains take half an hour more than 100 years later. Buses have long since taken the place of trams.

CHELMSFORD, HIGH STREET

Chelmsford has been the county town of Essex since the thirteenth century, and perhaps earlier. It was an important town during Roman times as it was fairly centrally placed on the great Roman way between London and Colchester. The Romans called it Caesaromagus.

WHITBY, STEPS LEADING TO THE PARISH CHURCH

These 199 steps impose a penance on the visitor to the church and abbey. Alongside the steps, which were originally wooden, runs the Donkey Road. St Mary's Parish Church at the top of the ascent was built about 1150.

KNARESBOROUGH, YORKSHIRE, ST ROBERT'S CHAPEL

Hollowed out of the solid rock some 500 years ago, this chapel is ten feet-deep in the cliff, its doorway guarded by a carving of a knight drawing his sword. St Robert was a hermit monk who came from Fountains in 1200. He lived in a cave farther down the river, and as a reward for penning deer (which had been eating the King's corn) was given as much land as he could plough in one day with a deer!

KNARESBOROUGH, DROPPING WELL

This petrifying spring has become a strange museum of 'stone' hats, birds, boots and baskets.
The water runs over the overhanging rock, on which the objects to be petrified are hung.
The water is heavily charged with limestone which coats the objects with a hard stone crust.

80

YORK, BOOTHAM BAR AND YORK MINSTER.
In Roman times, York was the capital of the northern province. It was the headquarters of the Sixth Legion under Hadrian and it was at York that Constantine was proclaimed as Caesar. Bootham Bar is a gateway in the city wall.

KINGSTOWN, ST MICHAEL'S RC CHURCH

Francis Frith was a staunch Quaker. Although he would not have approved of the imagery in Catholic, and even Church of England, buildings, he found them not only fine subjects for his camera but also lucrative postcard pictures, and many of his photographs were taken when he was travelling around to attend meetings of the Society of Friends.

NEWCASTLE, BLACK GATE

Medieval Newcastle was surrounded by massive walls two miles in circumference. The town, as in Roman days, was a military base for attacks against Scotland. The Black Gate is the main entrance to the Castle, and bears an inscription: 'This gateway was added to the royal castle of Newcastle upon Tyne by King Henry III in AD 1248'. It is said to have taken its name from Patrick Black, a seventeenth-century lessee. It now houses a splendid museum.

MANCHESTER SHIP CANAL, BARTON AQUEDUCT
When the Manchester Ship Canal was built a unique steel swing aqueduct was designed in order to allow ships to pass along the river below. The two ends of Barton Aqueduct can be sealed, and the complete 235ft length, full of water and weighing 1,450 tons, can be swung out of the path of approaching vessels.

Off the Beaten Track

UPWEY, WISHING WELL

The river Wey emerges here and begins its six mile run to Weymouth. At the well, according to local tradition, you should 'drink and your wish will come true'. Its origins are vague but it is recorded that George III visited the spot on his visits to Weymouth, between 1789 and 1805. It is still a tourist attraction.

FESTINIOG RAILWAY, TAN-Y-BWLCH STATION, CAERNARVONSHIRE
The Festiniog Railway (60cm gauge) still operates during the summer months between Portmadoc and Dduallt, a distance of 9½ miles. Tan-y-Bwlch is one of the intermediate stations on the line.

DOWNDERRY, CORNWALL, CAVE DWELLERS
Another uncharacteristic subject for Frith.

WHITBY, A SEA-URCHIN
This picture is not typical of Frith's work and is probably due to the influence of a contemporary, Frank Sutcliffe, who worked at Whitby and dedicated his life to recording genre scenes of the fishermen, farmers and tradesmen of this fishing port. This picture is more typical of Sutcliffe than it is of Frith.

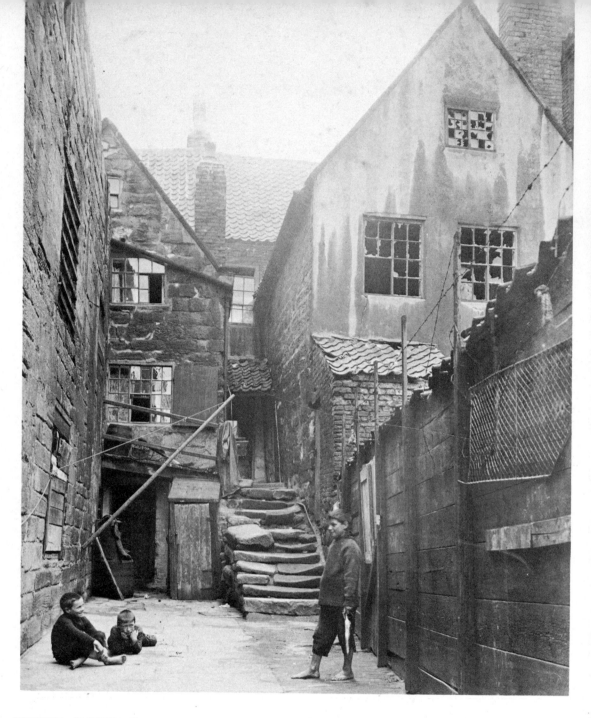

WHITBY, ARGUMENTS YARD

Another picture that owes a great deal in mood and content to Sutcliffe's portrayal of Whitby life. It is difficult to see how Frith could have made a commercial postcard from a dilapidated backyard, derelict buildings and barefooted boys. The yard was named after a family called Argument.

PORTLAND PRISON, CONVICTS

The old prison is no longer used for adult criminals (it is a Borstal training centre) but Portland stone is still quarried in vast quantities though without convict help. It is said that Inigo Jones changed the peninsula from a sheep grazing pasture to a quarry when he used the stone for the banqueting hall of the new Whitehall Palace. Wren also used it for St Pauls. The fashion spread and over 100,000 tons of Portland stone have been quarried in a year.

BLACKPOOL

The Blackpool Big Wheel was erected in 1896. It had 30 cars each one of which accomodated 30 passengers; the total weight of the wheel was 1,000 tons and the distance from ground to topmost girder 220 feet. The Big Wheel ceased to operate in 1928 and was broken up for scrap shortly afterwards.

90

TENBY, PEMBROKE, GRIFFITH'S TEMPERANCE HOTEL
Tenby looks alternately like a continental fishing port or a Victorian watering place. This is not surprising since Flemings were brought in during the time of Henry I to work the fish, wool and wine trade; while in the early nineteenth century Tenby was converted into an elegant resort by Sir William Paxton, a flamboyant Welsh magnate.

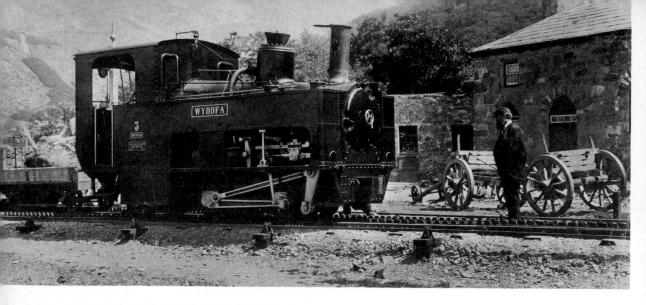

LLANBERIS, SNOWDON MOUNTAIN RAILWAY ENGINE
The Snowdon Mountain Railway (2ft 7½in gauge) was opened in 1896. This rack railway remains a popular tourist attraction and still uses much of the original equipment, including the locomotive shown in the photograph.

SNOWDON, THE SUMMIT
Once the Snowdon Mountain Railway was completed a trip to the summit was a popular tourist attraction, although most of the party in this photograph seem to be equipped for walking up.

WATCOMBE ROCKS

The coach and horse performs a double function—not only to transport Francis Frith and all his photographic impedimenta to the shooting location but also to act as a scale in the picture area. On this occasion Frith travelled light compared with his expeditions around Britain and the continent when the coach would be loaded with wife, seven children, nurse and coachman in addition to Frith and his camera, tripod, lenses, plates and accessories. In addition, space would have to be found for family necessities, such as food and clothes, and Frith's oil painting canvasses, easel and paints.

SIDMOUTH, SOUTH DEVON, THE GLEN, QUEEN VICTORIA'S NURSERY

Sidmouth first became a holiday resort in the early 1800s. But its really fashionable period was after 1819-20 when it was visited by the Duke and Duchess of Kent with their baby daughter, the Princess Victoria. They stayed at Woolbrook Cottage, now known as the Royal Glen. The duke died here in January 1820. Queen Victoria did not visit Sidmouth again.

LAXEY WHEEL AND SNAEFELL

The gigantic wheel is at Laxey on the Isle of Man and is regarded as one of the marvels of Manxland. It was built in 1854 by Robert Casement to pump the lead mines free of water. It has a circumference of 228ft and a diameter of 72½ft. Often known as the Lady Isabella Waterwheel, this pump could raise 250 gallons per minute from a depth of 1,800ft. The viewing platform above the wheel is 75ft from the ground and commands a fine view over Snaefell.

UNKNOWN

This picture is unique among Frith pictures in that it was not included in his index; also it was taken on a smaller format camera than was used for practically all his professional work. It is possible that this photograph was taken as a private picture, not intended for commercial use, possibly during a visit to the school of one of his sons.

On the Coast

DOVER CASTLE, QUEEN ELIZABETH'S POCKET PISTOL

This cannon, which is still kept in the grounds of Dover Castle, is believed to have been cast at the order of the Emperor Charles V and intended as a goodwill present for Henry VIII. However when relations between the monarchs deteriorated it was laid in store until it was presented to Queen Elizabeth I by the Orange party of the Netherlands. The barrel is beautifully decorated with a wealth of Renaissance ornament—vases, acanthus leaves, grotesques and allegorical figures. The cannon was more than just a presentation piece, however, and during the Civil War it formed part of Charles I's artillery train.

NEWLYN, CORNWALL

Newlyn is famous for its artists, its fish and its independence. In 1896, a few years after this picture was taken, Newlyn fishermen were angered that East Coast boats continued to fish on Sundays. So they boarded the 'Yorkies' as they came into harbour with their Sunday catch and threw it overboard—along with a local fish dealer who had been foolish enough to do business with the Sabbath breakers. The 'foreigners' were barred from using the harbour. Fierce fighting broke out and troops were brought in to restore the peace. Many Newlyn men went to prison, but they won their point. Sunday fishing from Newlyn was stopped.

NEWLYN, OLD FISHERWOMAN

98

GRIMSBY, FISH MARKET

Grimsby was, and still is, an important fishing port. The scene at fish auctions today is little different.

SHERINGHAM, NORFOLK (above and opposite)
Not so many years ago Sheringham was a mere handful of fishermen's cottages, and it has still managed to retain along its seafront the irregularity and lack of formality which has become synonymous with 'character'. Sheringham is still a fishing community—even the town arms displays 'a golden Lobster'. The boats have been motor-powered since the twenties.

The fishermen's cottages nowadays are less ramshackle, if less romantic, and not so closely intermingled with their gear as was the case in Frith's time.

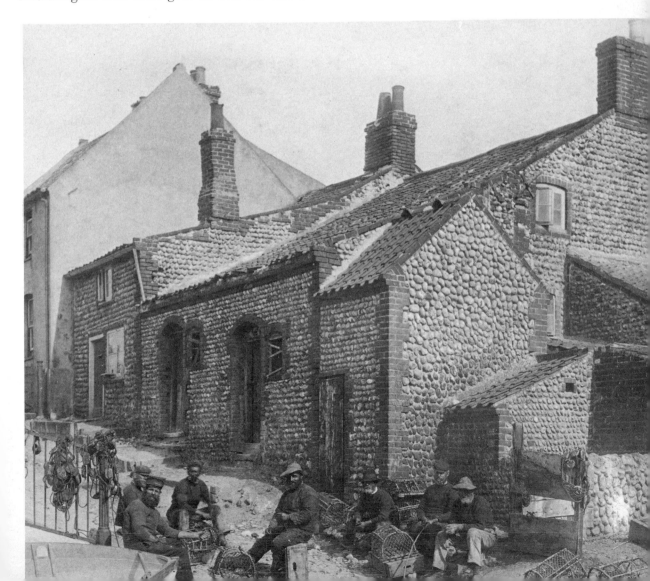

ST IVES

The first settlement on this stretch of the Cornish coast was called St Ia or Eia, after one of the missionaries from Ireland who landed there between 450 and 500. In the sixteenth century, the name was corrupted to St Ives. The 'junk' on the right might be of value today.

ST IVES FISHWIFE

PENZANCE

Until comparatively recently Penzance was the centre of a rich agricultural, fishing and mining area, though it did not develop beyond a market town until the railway arrived, following which a variety of attractions were provided for holiday-makers. Dick Renfree and Alma Hocking, the couple shown in this picture, were according to Frith 'well-known to Penzance visitors'.

PENZANCE PROMENADE BY MOONLIGHT

A beautiful Frith 'fake', comprised of at least three different prints pasted together into a montage, and the final result heavily retouched and hand-worked. The original is a soft blend of various tones and shades caused by different depths of brown in the several prints plus the several colours of airbrushing and inking.

CONWAY CASTLE

Another dramatic 'fake'. This time the result was achieved not by montage but by double printing. Two separate negatives were taken, one for the castle and foreground and the other underexposed for the sky effect. The negatives were subsequently printed on the same sheet of paper with the outlines of the castle carefully masked so that the clouds did not appear to float through the stone. This is a difficult and tedious job with the sophisticated equipment and fast papers in contemporary darkrooms. For Frith, with slow printing out papers, without an enlarger, the patience and skill required was considerable.

NEWQUAY

A sophisticated design for an early photograph. Note the profile in the lower left hand corner. This would have been no accident since Frith would be able to check the exact image area to be obtained on the plate by studying the camera's ground glass screen prior to making the exposure. It is significant that many young photographers today are rediscovering the contemplative approach with large format cameras since the miniature camera with bulk loads can so often lead to a collection of trivia. There is little or no commercial shipping in the harbour today.

HINDFIELD, HUTCOMBE HEAD
The best photographs work on two levels, as straight documents but with strange under-
currents that seep into pockets of the mind and remain as part of our experiences. This
photograph shows these characteristics.

BEXHILL ON SEA BEACH
Obviously a carefully posed picture—except perhaps for the dog in the foreground.

NEWQUAY, ON THE SANDS
Overlooking the bay is the Huer's hut once used as a lookout post from which the 'Huer' would watch for the approach of shoals of pilchards—a fish that epitomises Victorian high tea. On sighting the fish the 'Huer' would call through a megaphone-like trumpet 'Heva, Heva' and the cry echoed through the town as the fishermen rushed for their boats. By the turn of the century the practice was dying out, for the arrival of the railway changed the character of small fishing towns like Newquay. Sands and views rather than fish became the community's most valuable assets.

THE LYNTON AND LYNMOUTH CLIFF RAILWAY
The cliff railway was opened in 1890. The 3ft 9in gauge track is 900 feet long and worked by hydraulics.

Important Dates

1822   Born in Chesterfield, Derbyshire, of Quaker parents.

1828c Attends village school.

1834   Leaves home to attend Camp Hill Quaker boarding school in Birmingham.

1835   Death of elder sister, age fifteen.

1838   Holiday with parents in country farmhouse, on leaving school. Apprenticed to Sheffield cutlery firm.

1843   Illness. Travel with parents. Became committed Christian.

1845   Began wholesale grocery business with young partner in Liverpool. Corners Greek raisin crop.

1850   Established printing firm. Begins photography.

1856   Sells business. Year of idleness as 'gentleman' in London. First trip to Egypt. Sails from Liverpool to Alexandria, September.

1857   Returns to England, July. Second expedition to Egypt and Palestine begins, end of November.

1858   Returns to England, May. *Memorials of Cambridge* published, illustrated by by Frith.

1859   Starts photographic business in Reigate. Third expedition to Egypt, summer. Reaches Sixth Cataract of the Nile, further than any other photographer before him.

1860   Returns from Egypt. Marries Mary Ann Rosling, from a Reigate Quaker family. Lives at Church Fell, Reigate. Exploits photographs of Eastern travels in book form including:—

Cairo, Sinai, Jerusalem and the Pyramids of Egypt and *Egypt and Palestine*.

1862   Version of *The Holy Bible*, illustrated by Francis Frith. Publication of his stereoscopic pictures in book form: *Egypt, Nubia and Ethiopia*.

1864   Publication of *The Gossiping Photographer on the Rhine* and *The Gossiping Photographer at Hastings*.

1864c Birth of Alice. First of seven children: four boys and three girls, eighth child dying in infancy.

1865   Publication of *Hyperion*, illustrated with twenty-four photographs by Francis Frith.

1865c Francis Frith & Co built up into largest photographic publishers in the world. Moves to Brightlands, Reigate.

1877   Publication of *Evangelicalism*. Publication of *The Book of The Thames*, illustrated by Frith.

1885c Increasingly involved in painting, poetry and philosophy. Business takes up little time: managed by son Eustace. Moves to Walton Heath. Until his death winters in Cannes or San Remo, due to asthma and bronchitis.

1893   Publication of *The Quaker Ideal*.

1898   Dies at Cannes, buried in Protestant cemetery. Age, seventy-six.

1900   Posthumous publication of *The Autobiography of a Soul and other poems* by Francis Frith.

1935c Francis Frith & Co Ltd sells huge factory and moves to Cravenhurst, Raglan Road, also in Reigate.

1939   Eustace Frith dies; business sold to Mr A. F. Sargent.

1945   Mr Sargent's two sons, Frederick and Trevor, join Francis Frith & Co as managing directors.

1968   Sargents sell business to Pandora, stay on as consultants.

1971   Francis Frith & Co Ltd in liquidation.

Acknowledgements

I should like to place on record my sincere appreciation for the time and interest given to me by Francis Frith's four surviving grandsons. To Francis E. Frith of Wotten-under-Edge; to his brother Jasper Frith of Penrith; to Paul Crosfield of Broadway; and particularly to Claude Frith and his wife Nora, of Fletching. The latter deserve special thanks, for their patient and careful preservation of family photographs, diaries, manuscripts and books, and for their unstinting generosity in allowing me to draw on their collection for much of the contents of the text.

All the pictures in this book are reproduced from Frith's original prints—not one is a new print copied from an old photograph or made from the original glass plate. The fact that these prints have survived is not due, unfortunately, to the recognition of their worth by art museums, but to the alacrity with which the executives of a commercial company, Rothmans, arranged the purchase of the entire collection and its removal from the liquidator's bonfire at literally a few days notice. I am not only grateful to them for responding to the need with such enthusiasm and efficiency, but for allowing me complete access to the collection at all times, and for their encouragement to use many of their original prints for this book.

I would also like to express my appreciation to Paul Hill MSIA for the loan of some prints and to the following for providing information about the photographs included in this book:

J. N. Stebbing, District Librarian, Whitby; J. C. Buckhurst, Borough Librarian, Penzance; A. J. Charman, District Librarian, Haselemere; Dr G. Rolston; Diana M. Armstrong, Newquay Branch, Cornwall County Library; J. A. C. West, Chief Librarian, Weymouth and Melcombe Regis; A. J. Ricketts, Borough Librarian, Dover; Alan B. Stables, Branch Librarian, Sheringham; Valerie A. G. Allen, Branch Librarian, Tenby; Gilbert Turner, Borough Librarian, Richmond upon Thames; J. C. Powell, Borough Librarian, Maidenhead; J. P. Wells, City Librarian, Oxford; C. W. T. Huddy, Librarian, Evesham; J. G. Fisher, Reference Librarian, Chester; J. J. Eyston, the Mapledurham Estate Office; P. Dunderdale, Chief Librarian, Blackpool; Taunton Information Bureau; Devon County Library; Mrs Iris Mitchell of Cadgwith, Cornwall.

Index